DARRYL TELLES

we're
QUEER
AND WE SHOULD
BE HERE

THE PERILS AND PLEASURES OF BEING A GAY FOOTBALL FAN

D0550515

DARRYL TELLES

we're QUEER AND WE SHOULD BE HERE

THE PERILS AND PLEASURES OF BEING A GAY FOOTBALL FAN

MEREO
Cirencester

Mereo Books

1A The Wool Market Dyer Street Cirencester Gloucestershire GL7 2PR
An imprint of Memoirs Publishing www.mereobooks.com

We're queer and we should be here: 978-1-86151-827-9

First published in Great Britain in 2017
by Mereo Books, an imprint of Memoirs Publishing

Copyright ©2017

Darryl Telles has asserted his right under the Copyright Designs and Patents Act
1988 to be identified as the author of this work.

This book is a work of fiction and except in the case of historical fact any
resemblance to actual persons living or dead is purely coincidental.

A CIP catalogue record for this book is available from the British Library.

This book is sold subject to the condition that it shall not by way of trade or
otherwise be lent, resold, hired out or otherwise circulated without the publisher's
prior consent in any form of binding or cover, other than that in which it is
published and without a similar condition, including this condition being imposed
on the subsequent purchaser.

The address for Memoirs Publishing Group Limited can be found at
www.memoirspublishing.com

The Memoirs Publishing Group Ltd Reg. No. 7834348

Cover design & book artwork - Ray Lipscombe

The Memoirs Publishing Group supports both The Forest Stewardship Council®
(FSC®) and the PEFC® leading international forest-certification organisations. Our
books carrying both the FSC label and the PEFC® and are printed on FSC®-certified
paper. FSC® is the only forest-certification scheme supported by the leading
environmental organisations including Greenpeace. Our paper procurement policy
can be found at www.memoirspublishing.com/environment

Typeset in 12/18pt Century Schoolbook
by Wiltshire Associates Publisher Services Ltd. Printed and bound in Great Britain
by Marston Book Services Ltd, Oxfordshire

Printed on FSC approved paper

CONTENTS

Preface

Introduction

PART ONE: 2014-15

PART TWO: 2015-16

PART THREE – 2016-17

APPENDIX

PREFACE

This book has been my life for the three years I have taken to write it. It's the first book I have ever written, so please don't be too harsh in your criticisms. And thanks to all my friends and colleagues who have had to spend most of their time with me, during that period, hearing of my angst in completing it.

My love for memoirs and biographies has led me to this venture, and the best, as they say, are those that are as truthful as memory permits. So if I have made mistakes in terms of recollections of matches or details of games, please let me know.

I dedicate this book to the two most important people in anyone's life, Mum and Dad, who made the unfathomable decision to bring me into this world. What they did then one night in November 1963 has had reverberations, many of which are recollected in this book. I always point out that three momentous things occurred that month: the untimely death of President Kennedy, cut down in his prime; the beginning of the longest and most successful British television programme, *Doctor Who*; and lastly, the immaculate conception of my good self.

I have tried my utmost not to be impartial or discriminate in a book that is all about equality, respect for diversity and being fair and tolerant. I have failed. Any reference to that other team has been referred to as

'Woolwich' or 'the Gooners', so I apologise in advance to those who may be offended. That aside, I hope you enjoy this roller-coaster of a ride. I have certainly led an eventful life and as one reviewer suggested, I have packed a lot in into a short space of time.

To lovely Lucy, for listening.

INTRODUCTION

Imagine you're the only one of your kind, or at least you think you're the only one, hiding in a crowd of nearly 40,000 people. What are you hiding and why do you have to? You're hiding a secret, something you've only just told your closest friends, many of whom share that same secret, and can't understand why you place yourself in harm's way by going to such a place. That something hasn't gone down too well with those you hold most dearly – your own family. Yet through their sacrifice, you've managed to get a place at university, which will lead you to hold a job where you can talk about it and even teach and train others about it. You just can't tell everyone, especially not on Saturdays. To be more precise, every other Saturday, when your side is 'at home'.

Yet you still choose to be amongst that crowd. That crowd, if they knew what you got up to on the other Saturday, when the team plays away,would probably at best ask you to seek medical advice, or at worst, bludgeon you to death. For when Saturday comes, there can only be one place to be for a lifelong Spurs fan and that's White Hart Lane. Most of the crowd are white, and you stick out already because of your brown face. If they knew your other distinguishing charcteristic, they might not even let you through the gates. So you keep quiet – and just as well, for in your first game at home they're singing the sort of chants that make you feel unwelcome, and not only because of your colour – they just can't stand anyone who's a poof, an arse-bandit, a queer or a raving homosexual. And that's exactly what you are.

Your parents brought you here to get on in life, yet you're held back from trying to be who you are and enjoying what you like by the fear of being found out playing for the 'other side'. So you don't feel it's your home, and you can't imagine that there is anyone else who is gay in the same stadium.

In the middle of the 2012-13 football season, I nearly died. After what was billed as a routine operation for an abscess in my ear, I suffered from sepsis (blood poisoning) and collapsed at home. When the paramedic came, he took me straight to accident and emergency, where the consultant told me that if I had not been brought in, I probably wouldn't have survived the next 72 hours. With severe kidney failure, I spent the next three days in intensive care and a fortnight in hospital with four weeks recuperating at home. I spent some of that time doing a bucket list – detailing the things I should do before the next proverbial bus ran me over.One of these was to write a memoir, and what better place to set it than at White Hart Lane, where for the past 23 consecutive seasons, I had been a season ticket holder.

There are three things that really get me interested in life: football, sex and politics. They're what I know, what I love and what define me. I've been a Spurs fan for as long as I can imagine, and I've known that I prefer men sexually for probably the same period of time. It was back in my childhood that I knew what interested me and however much I tried to tell myself that being gay was a phase I was going through, it was here to stay. I couldn't imagine life without my beloved Spurs, just as I couldn't envisage denying that I loved men. And loving men in the late 1980s inevitably meant that if you wanted to be out, you had to be political.

Thatcher was still reigning in Downing Street and the notorious 'Section 28' law defined what she and her populist government thought of the LGBT(lesbian, gay, bisexual and trans) community. Local government, where I worked, was prevented by that law from providing council services tailored to us. We were deliberately meant to feel we were outsiders and should stay invisible, stigmatised because of our sexuality. In the midst of the HIV/AIDS pandemic, I was working with schools to address these issues and came across the blatant effects of this law. On one such occasion, I was on a local commercial station in London, Spectrum Radio, discussing the issue and the reporter prevented me from even using the term 'gay men' as he thought, wrongly as it happens, that Section 28 made it illegal for me to do so. Less than a generation ago, it seems that we were on a different planet from where we are now, but these were the times when there were few openly out gay actors, only one out gay MP and no sports stars, let alone football players, who were comfortable about being out. It was a time of fear and much loathing.

It is still a matter of conjecture when I actually became

a Spurs fan. It was, like my discovery that I was gay, some time during my years at a North London primary school. The first sticker album I collected, a rite of passage for any football fan of that era and one that I still possess, was 'The Wonderful World of Soccer' for the 1969-70 season. I recall being able to buy stickers for that by walking to and from school (sometimes carried by my brother) and using the money saved from the bus fare to buy the stickers. In that book I have marked the transfer of Jimmy Greaves from Spurs to West Ham United in exchange for the mercurial Martin Peters, so that's a sign of a preference for the Lilywhites. I think I was a Spurs supporter by the World Cup tournament of 1970, as you will discover later in this book. At school it was a choice between Arsenal and Spurs, the two local teams closest to Finchley, and I chose the latter.

My brother has a different tale to tell. Terry claims that on his specially-converted bike, which included a seat for me, we were stopped by two skinheads, one a Chelsea fan and the other a Spurs supporter, who asked us both what team we supported. I blurted out 'Spurs', whilst my brother said 'Chelsea'. It was the late 1960s and in those times, if you were young Asian kids, you usually tried to agree with what older white skinheads said. Whenever it was, I was a confirmed Spurs fan by the time we beat Aston Villa to claim the League Cup in 1971. I can definitely remember listening to that on the radio.

My first visit to the home of Spurs, White Hart Lane, didn't materialise until the 1978-79 season, which was our return to the top flight after only one season in Division Two. On the 14th November 1978 we played Brian Clough's Nottingham Forest, who were then the reigning champions. We lost 3-1 and all I can remember of that match is the crowd in the Paxton Road end where I was standing leading a chant of 'Brian Clough is a homosexual.' They had inferred this from his close friendship with Peter Taylor, his assistant coach. As we will find out later, this is an irony, given Clough's less than supportive reaction to one of his own players being outed. Given what I was feeling at that time about coming to terms with my own sexuality, I was more than a bit scared and put off by this chant. In the years preceding this, I had been taken by Terry to Stamford Bridge and had witnessed the racism displayed earnestly by some of the Chelsea fans. I really felt once again that I didn't fit in, and that I might as well give up my love for football if I wanted to stay out of the closet, or stay safe as a person of colour.

November 1978 also marked another significant turning point for me, for in that month I interviewed our local MP for the school magazine. This was no ordinary MP; she was the former Education Secretary and now Leader of the Tory opposition to James Callaghan's Labour Government – the aforementioned Margaret Thatcher. It was through this that my obsession with politics began. She was a diminutive Napoleonic sort of person, who I recall was bossing around senior teachers in the staff room to make us cups of tea.

For the rest of that season and beyond, it wasn't the terraces again. I spent my £5 weekly pocket money on a seat in the West Stand when I went next to the Lane the following season. In fact a fiver was enough for the seat, the return bus fare and a match day programme. I couldn't afford to go to away matches and didn't have any friends to travel with, so on the Saturdays when we were playing away from the Lane, I spent the fiver on going to some dive in Soho instead, to explore my sexuality. Wardour Street rather than White Hart Lane beckoned me. Even as a teenager, I looked old enough to spend that fiver getting into the dark caverns and labyrinths of cinemas, where I fulfilled my passions.

By the time the University of Warwick in Coventry beckoned in 1982, I was well and truly hooked on both Soho and the Spurs. With the latter I had even been fortunate enough to get a ticket for the FA Cup Final replay that year, when we beat Queens Park Rangers with a single goal from a Glenn Hoddle penalty. As for the Soho side of things, I had now found places closer to home in Finchley, where I could find men to befriend. I would regularly go to the Black Cap in Camden Town, the oldest gay pub north of the river. It would, in future, be the scene of our celebrations after the 1991 FA Cup final and then again in 1999, when we won the League Cup.

Whilst I was at university I did return to the Lane, most memorably for floodlit games on week nights in European cup tournaments, including, as you will discover later, the 1984 UEFA Cup final. Fortunately, I had left university by 1987 when we played Coventry City in their first FA Cup final. Thankfully I was nowhere near the city to witness their first-ever taste of glory, and our first-ever FA Cup final defeat. I had returned from university a grown man, comfortable with my sexuality and out to family, friends and work colleagues.

If ever there was a turning point in my life, it came two years later in 1989, when I replied to a box advertisement in *Gay Times*. for volunteers to help establish a Gay Football Supporters Network (GFSN). Fascinated by the concept, if a bit wary of what I was letting myself in for, I replied, and within a week I got an invitation to the next meeting and a copy of their newsletter. It was genuine. There was a dating service for sportswear fetishists, but in the main the newsletter contained articles about football, clubs, the issues facing gay fans and opportunities to meet fellow supporters of the team you followed. There was even a League table which showed that the two most widely supported clubs were Woolwich Arsenal (although the Gunners think they are the Pride of North London, they were originally from south of the river) and there in second place, the mighty Spurs.

I went along to my first meeting in the Salmon and Compasses pub in Chapel Street market in the Angel, Islington. Not perturbed by a couple of elderly men sitting at the bar in very tight shorts, the vast majority were just as they said – true football fans who like me were comfortable about their sexuality but not comfortable about the homophobia displayed at matches.

Within a year, and especially as the nation got hooked on Italia '90, the World Cup that summer, the group had rapidly grown to a national network of 350 members, with meetings also being convened in Glasgow, Manchester, Birmingham and Bristol. I took over our media profile by editing and dispatching the monthly newsletter. I also began to organise separate socials just for Spurs fans on Friday nights before our home games, at the King William IV pub in Hampstead. We even joined up with the Gay Gooners from Arsenal to have joint socials before the derby matches and most memorably, before the 1991 FA Cup semi-final.

Single-handedly Paul Gascoigne, probably the best player in the world during the 1990-91 season, took Spurs to their eighth FA Cup Final win, via a beating of the Woolwich, in that first semi-final between the two clubs, at Wembley Stadium. They had to settle for winning the League as we taunted them with cries of 'Where's your Double gone?' Surely this was the beginning of an era of Spurs dominance.

I remembered my history: 1971 and the League Cup win led to a flourish of finals until relegation in 1977 and a decade later, winning the FA Cup in 1981 led to a flurry of trophies, culminating in that win at the Lane of a European trophy in 1984. So why not become a season ticket holder? It was £79 for the whole season and through GFSN, I now had a group of gay friends to hang around with and the prospect of another European tour to boot. What could go wrong? With the Spurs group now attracting upwards of a dozen gay men, four of us decided to get season tickets for the 1991-92 season.

During the pre-season period, GFSN were chosen to appear in the Channel 4 programme strand for the LGBT community. 'Out' was the simple name of the series and our slot was on an issue entitled 'Personal Best', which featured GFSN members at one of our socials. The programme appeared on the 10th July 1991. It would be the first time I would appear on television revealing my sexuality. There was no turning back now.

Joining me as season ticket holders was Vince, who in his 40s, was just old enough to have seen the 'push and run' side that won the 1951 League Championship. He was now a disability rights advocate and had been a local councillor for Haringey. During his tenure, Haringey became the first authority in the country to positively promote LGBT issues in schools. Overnight Vince became a national celebrity as the Government introduced the aforementioned Section 28 as a result. Rather than complying to this edict, he resigned as a councillor. Vince is a loyal Spurs fan, born and bred in Tottenham.

Then there was David, in his 30s and born in Blackpool, who went to university in Newcastle and had moved down to London to come out. And last but not least there was Fraser, just a couple of years older than me, who was also from up north and had been to university in Canterbury. As a social worker, he had met Vince whilst working in Haringey and had also, like David, become a Spurs fan in the eighties.

As for me, I was born in Kenya to Goan parents from India and had lived in Finchley since 1969, when I was five.

Inow worked in equal opportunities, so was out to both work colleagues and family, yet couldn't, until meeting these three, come out at the Lane.

There was protection and validation being in a group, and watching matches together would hopefully mean we could be ourselves.As we will discover, there would be much laughter, some sadness and above all, just an overwhelming sense of relief that we could be open about who we were and what we got up to.

PART 1

✳

2014/15

CHAPTER 1

LATE FOR THE KING

✳

MAY 2014

It was like being a child in a tuck shop with an unlimited facility to devour your favourite sweets. Wembley Stadium hosted the 20th anniversary celebration of Kick it Out, the grass roots organisation that had been formed to eradicate racism from the beautiful game. I felt privileged to have been invited as one of the co-chairs of the newly-formed Proud Lilywhites LGBT fan group, which had been established by Spurs a few months ago and had its first AGM the week before. Our legitimacy as LGBT fans had finally been recognised by the club we loved.

About twenty Spurs fans, including me, had responded to an advert on the Spurs website about the formation of an LGBT supporters group. This was in response to a campaign which I had helped promote a couple of seasons earlier, about how homophobia was allowed to exist in the grounds at matches through verbal insults and prolonged chanting directed at some individuals, and the lack of recognition of the issue in anti-discrimination regulations. For example, fans could be banned for racist insults but not homophobic ones. Arsenal became the first club to set up an official LGBT fan group in 2013, the Gay Gooners, so as a result Spurs were playing catch-up.

Our launch took place earlier this year, with a feature in the match day programme and a photo opportunity with club legend and ambassador Ledley King before the start of our Round of 32 Europa League match at home to Ukrainian club, Dnipro, managed by our ex-manager Juande Ramos. I arrived very early for the launch and took my time having a pre-match meal. We were due to meet at 5pm in the West Stand reception area and I got to the gates at 4.45, but infuriatingly it was just at the same time as the coach carrying our visitors arrived. I didn't get past the queue at the gate until after 5 and I was dismayed to be told that the club only wanted the first ten arrivals to join Ledley on the pitch – I was no 11. I was disappointed to say the least, but I enjoyed the hospitality of the club as I watched the game with all my fellow LGBT friends. Never mind, I was told, there will be plenty of other opportunities.

So this was one of them. I was going to enjoy this evening at Wembley Stadium come what may, and it more than lived up to my expectations. Spurs had grabbed table

2, right next to the top table. Sitting with me were former players Gary Mabbutt and Garth Crooks, plus staff from the club's Community Foundation and representatives from the Disabled Supporters' Association. I was reminded of the time Fraser had written to Gary, who was then the club captain, inviting him to one of our GFSN nights at the gay pub in Hampstead. Gary replied that he was busy but wished our group success. Garth Crooks was just like he is on the television, excited, loud and enthusiastic.

Before the formal proceedings began, I used the time to mingle with some of my childhood heroes, the pioneers of black British footballers, who had blazed a trail for many others to follow. Amongst those I was fortunate enough to talk to, were Cyrille Regis, the ex-West Bromwich Albion player who I had seen play for Coventry City whilst I was at university. Regis was part of the so-called 'Three Degrees' who played at the Hawthorns, along with Brendan Batson and the late Lawrie Cunningham. The patronising nicknames given to black players in the 1980s have always annoyed me. They were meant to be affectionate, but black players were often treated like novelties then, rather than professionals. When Cyrille went to Highfield Road, the Coventry fans nicknamed him 'Smokin' Joe' after the American heavyweight boxer Joe Frazier.

I also met with the organisers of a petition to give a posthumous Victoria Cross to Walter Tull, Tottenham Hotspur's first black player, who left football to be an officer in the trenches of the First World War. He was also the League's first black outfield player to appear in the top flight. Commissioned in the army and becoming the first black officer in 1917, he tragically died a year later.

I talked to Chris Powell, who was one of the first black managers at a senior level in the professional game. It was just like talking to a friend you had known for many years. Chris was from Tooting in South London and knew the road my godfather had lived in. It was great to see how easy he was to talk to, and then he surprised me. "So if you're a Proud Lilywhite, you must be on the Spurs table?" he said. "Yes" I replied. Was he going to make a pitch for the vacant role of Head Coach, I wondered? He whispered into my ear, "I am a massive Spurs fan, is that Mabbsy on your table?" Again I gave a tentative nod. "Can you introduce me please?" Chris nervously said. "He's my boyhood hero and I've never met him." Apparently Chris used to travel to Spurs on the bus and watch games from the Shelf. I duly introduced the player to his mentor. I was dumbstruck; which planet am I now on that I get to introduce Chris Powell to Gary Mabbutt? Maybe one day, in the not too distant future, as a gay supporter, I would be able to come to an event where I could empathise with out gay professionals.

Sitting on table 1 next to ours were all the dignitaries who were going to speak on stage. After our meal, there was a keynote speech by the former Prime Minister, Gordon Brown. I had never rated him as PM. At first, like most of the country, I had warmed to him when he was elevated to the role in 2007, simply because he was someone other than Tony Blair. However, as the financial crash of the following year set into a deep recession, he became known as Mr Bean rather than Superman, in the words of one opposition MP. His speech therefore was an utter revelation. For once he spoke from the heart, and his was the most robust denunciation of racism that I had heard for a long time. I congratulated him personally and thought what a difference it might have made if he had shown that charisma and passion during the election he had lost in 2010.

Ambling to his table after his speech was one of his predecessors as Labour leader, Neil Kinnock, who was accompanied by Malky Mackay, the Cardiff City manager. Kinnock didn't look at all a well man; his face was blotchy, bloated and bright crimson in colour. Mackay looked totally uninterested in everything and was for the whole evening glued to his mobile phone, continually texting.

Brown's speech was followed by a round-table discussion with the three wise men who had founded Kick it Out in 1994. Hosted by the ebullient Crooks, there was Herman Ouseley, who was now a member of the House of Lords; David Davies, who was at the Football Association when it was formed, and Gordon Taylor, the Chief Executive of the Professional Footballers' Association.

When Crooks started to speak Kinnock turned round to Mackay, who was still avidly texting, and said loudly, "I nearly got him to stand for us you know in a by-election." Mackay didn't reply, but I knew exactly what election Kinnock was talking about. It was in 1989 when I lived in Brixton and it led to a letter of mine appearing in *The Guardian*. I was against Kinnock's attempts to get a Labour candidate imposed on Vauxhall, one of Brixton's constituencies, rather than let the local party select a local candidate. They had asked Crooks and a multitude of black professionals, who all turned them down except for one, a television reporter, who had to stand down when it was discovered he was a closeted 'homosexual'. Kate Hoey was chosen instead and is still the MP nearly 30 years later.

Also on the politico table were Yvette Cooper and her husband, the Shadow Chancellor Ed Balls, who both had ambitions to be future Labour leaders. Like Malky Mackay however, they spent the entire night tweeting and texting. They only seemed to be interested when an opportunity for a selfie arose, after the winner of the Voice, the BBC's latest talent show, turned up.

Not for Malky Mackay though – he just kept texting, oblivious to what was happening around him. Just a month later he would end up at a FA disciplinary hearing for sending racist, homophobic and anti-Semitic texts. Maybe he should have listened to what was being said that night.

CHAPTER 2

PUBS AND POCHETTINO

✳

JUNE/JULY 2014

Spurs ended the season in a disappointing position. Although we had claimed a spot in the Europa League for the fifth season running, we were in 6th place. So yet another sacking of our coach, this time Tim Sherwood, after barely a season in charge, followed and another new appointment was made. At least this one came at the end of the season and not midway through. Mauricio Pochettino was the second manager we had poached from Southampton and the 14th in total since 1991. Compare this to the five (Bill Nicholson, Terry O'Neill, Keith Burkinshaw, David Pleat and Peter Shreeves) I had known as a supporter between 1970 and the nineties.

After winning the FA Cup as manager, Terry Venables became Chief Executive and appointed first Peter Shreeves, for his second spell in charge and then a double act to replace himself in the dug-out – Doug Livermore and ex-goalie Ray Clemence. It was never clear who exactly was selecting the team whilst Terry was still with us. When Venables' relationship with club chairman Alan Sugar disintegrated, Sugar tried to pacify fans with his appointment of Ossie Ardiles. He lasted just over a season before being replaced by Gerry Francis. Once touted for the England position, it seemed for a while that we had finally found someone worthy of being our manager. However, his reliance on ageing players and a stark inability to keep them fit led to him staying just three seasons.

We had tried a double-act, an ex-legend, a young bright thing, and now we went abroad and found Christian Gross from Switzerland. He lasted just a year. Unable to dust off the caricature of an absent professor, and more crucially gain a work permit for his assistant, he was replaced by a seasoned professional, George Graham. The ex-Chelsea and Woolwich player, who had also managed the Gooners, didn't go down well with the club and when Sugar sold up to Daniel Levy in 2001 the new Chairman curried favour with the fans by bringing in legend Glenn Hoddle, much like Sugar's first trick when appointing Ossie. Again he barely lasted three seasons, which was now becoming the norm for managerial appointments at the Lane.

David Pleat managed the club for a second time for a whole season whilst the Board scouted for a replacement.

Briefly we were excited by the next appointment, Jacques Santini, the French team coach who came to us with most of his coaching staff from managing the national side in Euro 2004. He lasted less than six months, much shorter than the whole year it had taken to find him!

Out of all this mess came Martin Jol, a Dutch coach, who for his passion and commitment to Tottenham's style of playing won the hearts and minds of all supporters. He lifted the club from a top ten side to a top six one and the way he was cruelly axed during a Europa League match against the Spanish side Getafe in 2007 led many to shout for the next change to be in the boardroom, rather than on the bench. After the match, when Jol was finally told of his sacking, I and several other fans queued up to vent our anger by being interviewed by television reporters. I featured on the local ITV London news that night. Of all the dismissals, that was the only one that really hurt and his replacement, Juande Ramos, seemed more interested in winning cups than securing our league position. He lasted only 18 months before our worst start to a top-flight season led to Harry Redknapp taking the hot seat in 2008. His contract wasn't renewed four years later despite two FA Cup semi-final appearances and taking the club to its first campaign in the Champions League. Then two seasons ago we appointed Andre Villas Boas, the ex-coach of Chelsea, who lasted another 18 months, and last season we were in the hands of caretaker Tim Sherwood, who although started very well, finished badly. And so 13 appointments later, we end up with Mauricio Pochettino; a hybrid of all previous managers, I suppose. He was an ex-player who was young enough to still empathise with the players, and from abroad, which seemed to be the mantra, with Sir Alex Ferguson at Manchester United excepted, to guarantee success. I felt like my Dad,who when he doubted the wisdom of change used to shrug and say, 'We will see'.

If it was all change with the team and coaching staff, it also felt like a new beginning with the Proud Lilywhites first full season ahead of us. There were three choices for the name of the LGBT supporters' group, and they were put to a vote. Along with the one finally chosen, the Proud Lilywhites, we short-listed Tottenham OutSpurs and Out at Spurs. We also designed a new rainbow flag, which gloriously would appear in the stadium at the start of the new season, with a version of it for a pin badge. We were all set to go, and had even set our own targets for membership, which we wanted to reach 100, by the next AGM.

Our first public event would, like the GFSN socials I used to attend all that time ago, be a pub social. There would be one major difference, and it is worth reflecting upon on how things have changed. In the 1990s when GFSN was formed we were still into self-organisation. I know that term is jargon, but I can't find a better one to describe it. In a sense we wanted to provide a safe space for gay fans to be themselves away from the strains of being closeted on the terraces. So we met in exclusively gay bars, socialised after watching football together in gay clubs and even one Christmas social relaxed with a gay cabaret, including a male stripper. Now the emphasis was about being more open, visible and out to the rest of society and more importantly, with other supporters. We had met with the Tottenham Supporters' Trust, something we had never done previously. The closest we had got to the then unrecognised

Tottenham Independent Supporters Association was writing an article which appeared in their fanzine, asking fans to consider not chanting the homophobic Campbell song. The lyrics of that song aren't worth repeating, but it does include reference to hanging and HIV infection. As I was to learn later, this hadn't gone unnoticed by the club officials.

So the Proud Lilywhites' first outing would be to a local pub, the Goose in Wood Green. We had chosen this location to see the Belgium v Russia World Cup match. Many of our squad players came from Belgium, and there was an understandable feeling that the homophobic laws recently enacted in Russia would make this the ideal match to watch. Spurs donated some prizes, including a team shirt signed by some of the players and a ticket for a VIP stadium tour. The Goose was also where the London Romans football team met after club matches. The team, made up of mostly gay players, were the reigning GFSN Cup holders. Since we had left GFSN, the organisation had largely concentrated on playing football rather than being supporters. It had grown in size to encompass its own national league and teams like Stonewall had made an impact abroad. They had also allowed non-gay players to play as long as they were comfortable and supportive of the anti-homophobia ethos of the teams. This was a far cry from what the GFSN had initially been established for and now with hindsight, I'm not sure that I was right to be hostile to such a change.

The event would also be used to promote the unfurling of our new club banner, which would adorn the stadium at home matches next season. It really only dawned on me at half-time that here we were, about 20 out LGBT fans in the middle of North London in our football shirts and with our rainbow banner in a straight working-class pub. How far we had come.

As we packed away the banner and said our farewells until the new season began, I remembered another pub. Fifteen years before, on the 30 April 1999, the London nail-bomber left a device in the Admiral Duncan pub in Soho's Compton Street, the heart of the gay village in London. Three people died, including a pregnant woman who had just got married. Many more were badly injured. The bomb followed explosions in Brick Lane, targeting the Bengali community in East London, and then in Brixton market, centre of London's African-Caribbean community. These were all a dreadful terrorist assault on multi-cultural, diverse London. At the time I was Chair of the Lesbian and Gay Coalition Against Racism, and we organised a demonstration along with colleagues from the National Assembly Against Racism, to take place in Brixton at the weekend. The bomb was clearly designed to make us scared – to make us go back in the closet. If this was the intention, then the exact opposite happened, as we had a GFSN social that very same night as the Soho nail-bomber struck.

By now GFSN socials had been moved to the larger venue of Central Station, a gay pub in King's Cross. We had an excellent relationship with the proprietors and they had readily converted their top floor bar into a sports lounge, which meant we could access viewing satellite TV coverage of football matches. When we met, there was a feeling of unease and sadness, and we noticed that security, always present before because of the threat of homophobic attacks, had been stepped up quite a few notches. However, the mood soon changed to one of defiance when the television cameras arrived and along with David, I was interviewed on the BBC news. I publicised the march the following night. What I didn't quite realise is that the BBC had advertised my mobile phone number on their website and it kept ringing throughout the night with people wanting further details of when and where the demonstration was taking place.

One of the immediate aims with the Soho bombing, where the injuries were far more severe and the impact of the devastation greater than the other two, was to establish an appeals fund. I met with Conservative donor Ivan Massow to establish this. and my friend Paul Macey, who was working for *The Voice* newspaper, joined the Appeals Fund Committee. Later that month we organised a rally outside the Admiral Duncan pub and I spoke along with Peter Tatchell and putative London Mayor Ken Livingstone. Out of that wreckage, a more united, more tolerant and much stronger London rose for the next century.

So I shouldn't really have been surprised when we unfurled our banner. It slowly dawned on people who we were and where we were – a gay Spurs supporters group – and it was heart-warming in a local Spurs pub to receive such warm applause. A middle-aged woman said rather loudly, "Ooh I should tell my son Jack to join, he thought he was the only one!" That for me made the day despite a dour 0-0 scoreline.

This was why we were there, to be out, loud and proud.

CHAPTER 3

50 YEARS

✴

AUGUST 2014

So I had reached my 50th birthday still intact, just about! That meant that as I approached my 24th consecutive season as an East stand season ticket holder at the Lane, I had spent the best part of half my life watching Spurs. And of course that didn't include the on-off appearances between 1978 and 1991. If you recall, I said that my first season ticket in the Shelf, where we stood for the last season when standing was allowed, cost a mere £79. Today that price would probably get you into one Premiership game and a Europa League tie with enough spare for programmes. Now my season ticket is a tenner short of £1000.

Of course my love of Spurs pre-dates that first appearance on the Paxton Road terraces in 1978, as I watched and listened to the club on the television and radio from at least 1970. If my love for Spurs began at such an early age, then when did my sexuality come to the fore?

Primary school, September 1970. It was a cold wet day, and my Mum cried as she left me for my first day in a new setting. I was the last to enter the door of Infants 1, my class in St Theresa's primary school in Finchley. The teacher welcomed me to the class and asked Danny McCarthy to mentor me for the day. There was an audible groan from Danny.

And then I fell in love, or at least had my first crush. Danny was the 'lad' of the class, great at football, full of charisma and the best-styled mullet haircut, in the whole school – just like the footballers of those times. I followed him around for the day in awe and learnt a few swear words which didn't go down too well at home. The following week I was moved to another desk as a result. Yet those feelings would still remain, and I would also have crushes on other boys in the school, however much I tried to think of girls.

Bishop Douglass Secondary School followed five years later, and as I reached puberty my sexuality was determined to be let out. For me, being gay wasn't a lifestyle choice; it just seemed to be in my genes, a natural attraction that I couldn't fight, however much I tried. But that certainly didn't mean I was going to tell anyone about these feelings, well not at school at least.

A family friend managed the Odeon cinema in Muswell Hill, and every week I would hop on the 102 bus to see the latest film, careful to ensure he wasn't around if I wanted to see an AA release (for those over 15). I had no problem getting in and was rarely asked for any identification to verify my age. Next door was a newsagent's with the most lurid top shelf sex magazines possible. This was before the days such magazines had to be covered up. Only the first time I bought a gay sex magazine was I asked whether I was over 18, and thereafter I could buy them whenever I could afford to.

Paul was two years younger and in the fourth year when we met, whilst I was in the sixth form. He was camp, had a circle of exclusive female friends and was keen on dance classes. He took some flak for all three and I recall several times at lunchtimes joining in with the name-calling he received. He always took it on the chin, either moving to another table or staying silent. My heartbeat always used to rise if I had to sit on his table, as I would have to join in the barracking to cover my own leanings. If I felt sad with myself, I didn't let myself wonder how Paul must have felt.

So getting pornography was pretty easy, as it is for young people today. However actually doing it, engaging in sex, was more challenging. I couldn't strike up relationships with anyone at school. There was only Paul and perhaps a couple of others I thought might be gay, but what if I tried it on with them and they weren't? I would be subjected to a torrent of abuse.

The staff weren't helpful either. My form teacher, for example, continually baited me that I wasn't English, and because I was useless at Physical Education and Games, he delighted in mocking my sporting attempts. In health education classes, we were specifically not told about three things: contraception, abortion and homosexuality.

Considering that the absence of the first (contraception) led to the prevalence of the second (abortion) and that doing the third (masturbating) could avoid the first two, this seemed to me illogical, but then I was being taught in a Catholic school.

All this meant that if I wanted relationships which went beyond the fantasies of pornography, I had to break the law. The age of consent for men was 21. I would have to wait seven years, and then only be able to do it in a private home with no others present. I had no intention of waiting.

About a mile from where I lived I heard that there was a 'cruising ground'. For the uninitiated, this is parlance for a recreation area, woodland or park where men meet other men for sex. Near to the outdoor swimming pool in Finchley was an area of natural beauty, and yes after dusk there were some beauties to be found. On one occasion I met a radio DJ from one of the coolest pirate stations around. I so wanted to tell someone but couldn't. He was in his mid-20s and still not out. As I was to discover, this was not unusual with people I met. Ironically he had a shop on Tottenham's High Road.

Another time I met Paul and we started a relationship. He never mentioned the taunts I had spouted at him. I think he was so used to them that he may not even have realised that I was one of the perpetrators. We would regularly meet in the woods, and then once we met at my home after school. It was the first time I had sex in my own bed, and I was so anxious about it that I never saw Paul again. Many times he would knock on my front door after school and I wouldn't answer, petrified that others would realise we were having a relationship.

As I looked round the tables of my guests gathered for my birthday bash, I was pleased that even a couple of fellow pupils from my secondary school had made it. On other tables were friends from university, where I would finally come out in my last year, and of course the friends I had made from the LGBT community since then. My mum was there, along with my brother and his family. The evening was another tick off my bucket list: to host a stage show. I had hired the Komedia club in Brighton and decided to do an old-fashioned light entertainment show. Patrick, a friend who had studied acting in drama school, joined me on stage for comedy sketches, Mitch's son played the piano and we even had a professional singer. Everyone seemed to enjoy it, and as ever, I enjoyed being the centre of attention.

On one of the tables were my newest friends from the Proud Lilywhites. I had bonded closely with the wife of the group's lesbian co-chair, Monica. She would be 50 next month and we shared similar experiences and saw things in the same political light. She knew her football, and as well as being a Spurs supporter, she had been a player for Hackney Women's team. She and her partner, Chris, had become the first LGBT couple to have a civil partnership at White Hart Lane. Monica was so pleased when I asked her to join me on stage. I had asked several people, one from each stage of my life and she was truly honoured.

As we left the club I thought of Paul and wondered how he was getting on. It would have been more truthful if I had invited him there, so that I could apologise in person and own up to all my friends and family about how harsh I had been. For all my campaigning since then for equal rights and diversity, Paul had been out at such an early age and had taken all the name-calling and abuse hurled at him.

Monica suddenly came up to me. "I just wanted to say how nice it was for you to invite me. We've only known each other six months," she said. She could tell that something was bothering me. "Whatever your feeling right now," she said. "Remember that tonight there was so much love in this room for you." It was probably one of the kindest things anyone has ever said to me, but I couldn't help reflecting on my treatment of Paul all those years ago and feeling that I was unworthy of all this praise and attention.

We started the season with two London derby wins, 1-0 in the opening match against West Ham away and 4-0 against Harry Redknapp's QPR at the Lane. In the Europa League play-off we beat AEK Limassol of Cyprus 5-1 on aggregate over two legs. The month ended badly though, with a 3-0 reverse to Liverpool at home.

CHAPTER 4

PATRONS AND PATRONAGE

✳

SEPTEMBER 2014

Spurs had a stumbling September drawing with Sunderland away 2-2 in the Premiership. This was followed by a 0-0 draw in Serbia against Partizan Belgrade in the Europa League. Two home matches followed – a loss against the Baggies in the Premiership followed by a comfortable 3-1 win against Nottingham Forest in the League Cup. We drew with Gunners at the Emirates 1-1.

One idea we had to boost the visibility of the Proud Lilywhites was to sign up a patron – a key supporter or celebrity who people would recognise and who would give us credibility when applying for funding for activities. Spurs were quite generous in initially providing us with prizes for raffles and free use of their meeting rooms, but we needed to show willing in matching this through our own fund-raising efforts.

We initially approached Ian Thorpe, the much-decorated Olympic swimmer from Australia, who had come out as gay a few months ago. He had previously featured in the match day programme as a keen Spurs fan. We finally got through, after several attempts, to chat to his agent down under. He didn't seem keen: "Ian has received so many offers since the summer and he's inundated. I'll let you know if he's interested." He didn't even seem to know that Ian was a Spurs supporter, and we never heard from him again.

I had a further thought and suggested Dan Gillespie-Sells, lead singer of the band The Feeling. He was Vince's nephew and I had met him at one of the band's gigs at the Hammersmith Apollo. I'm not noted for my knowledge of the music scene, in fact that was one of the few gigs I had ever attended. The Feeling were at the time a class act, and Dan was an out gay man. Unfortunately he knew nothing about football, and although Vince had taken him to a few games, he declined my offer to help us out.

The club then approached us with their own suggestion and Helen Richardson-Walsh, the Olympian hockey player, was mentioned. Although I must confess that I didn't recognise the name straight away, I warmed to the idea of getting help from the bronze medal winner at the 2012 London Olympics. She was just recovering from a nasty injury and we were invited to meet her before the upcoming

Beskitas match, our first home tie in the group stage of the Europa League. I didn't expect to be feted in quite such a manner, as when we arrived we were told we had been given a match day box to meet her for the entire match. I was slightly fazed by this patronage and felt a tad guilty for leaving my friends to watch the tie from the coldness of the stands just below us. Well someone has to do it I suppose!

Accompanied by Monica and her partner Chris, we were in a box with Helen and her brother, and the five of us hit it off immediately. Helen knew her Spurs history and was delighted to promise her support to the Proud Lilywhites within a few minutes of meeting us, which was a relief as we could then settle down to watch the match.

In the next box, or 'executive lounge', as hospitality grandly calls them these days, was Nacer Chadli, who had been rested for the game. He kindly signed my programme, which gave us another prize to auction at an event. I realised later that he was the first first-team player I had come out to.

Helen was keen to find out what our aims and objectives were. Fortunately we had spent September surveying our members and the growing number of supporters for our Facebook page, for which we wanted to reach 500 likes by the end of the season. Broadly speaking our aspirations for the Proud Lilywhites fell into three categories. First, we wanted to have fun – to have socials and provide a welcoming place both at the ground and before matches for LGBT fans to meet. We would do this by hosting a table in the Members Lounge. Then we wanted to be educational – we wanted to explain to other supporters why they should make the Lane more welcoming for LGBT fans. I kept saying: 'We want to make Spurs the most LGBT friendly club in the Premiership.' Many LGBT people had negative and hostile attitudes to football and the gay media always tended to highlight the bad things about the game and exaggerate occurrences of homophobia, which put off a lot of people from attending. So education was a two-way process, not just with existing fans but in selling the club to potential new audiences. Last but not least was the campaigning strand; by supporting events such as the Football v Homophobia month or the regular Kick it Out season of action, we wanted to get a message out of visibility and inclusion.

The match itself was another bore draw. I could sense, even tucked away in this exclusive box, that the crowd were getting restless. Pochettino had changed the style of play of the team, with more emphasis on work rate and passing rather than flowing attacks, which some purists demanded was the Tottenham style. We would have to grit our teeth and watch it and just hope that given time, we could reach the top four again, which we had done only twice in Premiership history.

The highlight for me was when we were surprised by two Spurs legends who came through the executive lounge – Paul Allen from our side in the late 1980s and early 1990s, and John Pratt, a stalwart from my childhood in the 1970s. I said to John: "I know your cousin." John, slightly fazed by this admission, replied, "That must be David." "Yes that's the one," I said and gave him a cheeky grin.

Monica tackled me on the issue just after I had taken a photo with him and Paul. "So how well do you actually know this David?" she asked. Rather camply, I replied, "It will be in my memoirs one day."

As I said my goodbye to Monica, I looked forward to her 50th birthday party later in the month, but there was no party. Just before it was due to happen, Monica took her own life. We were all stunned and deeply saddened for her partner Chris and for Monica's family, who flew in from New Zealand for her funeral. Words can't describe my feelings at the immense loss I felt, and it was hardly surprising that there were hundreds of people at her cremation in Golders Green. She had meant so much to me and had made such a lasting impact in such a short space of time to all of us in the Proud Lilywhites.

Our first event had been a social, so we now turned to campaigning, with a public meeting to be held in the Bill Nicholson lounge at White Hart Lane at the end of the month. It would be in the week of our next tie in the Europa League, the home match against Asteras Tripolis from Greece. The week had been designated a Week of Action against Racism and discrimination by UEFA and their partner organisation FARE (Football Against Racism in Europe). FARE was a community organisation that advised UEFA on disciplinary incidents related to racism and discrimination that occurred during matches. It did this by sending a series of observers to matches to look for any displays of racism or discriminatory behaviour by supporters at matches, ranging from the display of offensive right-wing flags to hateful chanting or acts of violence. I had successfully applied to them for funding to help us organise our event to cover the costs of our speakers, some publicity and catering at the event. FARE was keen to promote initiatives against homophobia, as it had just started its own work in this field.

The speakers for our meeting were Helen, our new patron, myself, Jo Tongue, from Women in Football, and Troy Townsend from Kick it Out. I was in awe of Troy, not only as he was the father of Andros, who had broken into both our side and the England team with such flair, but also because he was totally unassuming and wholly committed to his role as the Education Manager at Kick it Out, where he trained academy players against discrimination. More than 80 people attended the meeting and we had good media coverage before and after the event from *Gay Times, Diva* and *The Guardian*.

Chris spoke emotionally at the beginning to introduce us all. In the presence of Monica's family, who were still there and had come to the meeting, I also paid my own tribute to her, which led to a dignified minute's silence to remember her memory.

The key topic on the night was what the reaction of supporters, club officials and fellow players would be when and if a top-flight footballer came out. Disappointingly, I thought, Troy gave a frank but pessimistic assessment, saying that it wouldn't happen in his lifetime because of the fear of the reaction from players and supporters alike. I took exception to this and criticised this approach —rather harshly, with hindsight: "If we are sitting here in our anti-discrimination world and we can't be more positive than that, then what chance does anyone have to come out?" I proclaimed. "And I don't believe we would stand for a bad reaction now, maybe ten or twenty years ago, but not now. There would be enough of us on the terraces who were LGBT or had friends and family that were out to stamp out any bad reaction."

This brought applause in the room, but I don't think Troy was happy at how I had said that, and I don't think he has ever forgiven me.

After our draw against Besiktas, we got a much-needed narrow 1-0 win against Pochettino's old club Southampton at home in the League. Facing the reigning Champions away, we went down 4-1 to Manchester City. We demolished the Greek side 5-1 at the Lane with Kane scoring a hat-trick and a rabona from Lamela. At the end of the month though, our disappointing form in the Premiership continued, with a 2-1 loss to Newcastle United.

CHAPTER 5

POLICING IS PAINFUL

✳

OCTOBER 2014

Our last match in October would prove to be a testing one for the Proud Lilywhites and a painful one for me. We were drawn at home to Brighton and Hove Albion in the third round of the League Cup. I had moved down to live in Brighton in 2011, disenchanted with London. The capital city had become cold and unfriendly and I was wasting away in Barking. When my employer moved its offices from Bermondsey to London Bridge, I was within an hour or so's commute from the seaside alternative. As I would discover, Brighton had all the bonuses of living in London and few of the disadvantages. It was more neighbourly, as diverse as London and was known for its acceptance of the thriving LGBT community. It also had a well-supported football team that had built an impressive new stadium near the university campus in Falmer, on the outskirts of the city.

I went to the opening match of the Amex Stadium in the summer of 2011 as the Seagulls played Spurs in a preseason friendly. The fact that we won is irrelevant – it was the hostile atmosphere that shocked me. Because of the sizeable LGBT community in Brighton, there were numerous unsavoury chants from the Spurs fans in the end I was in, directed at the home crowd. Now some may see it as banter and when it's written down here it does look as nothing more than a bad joke: 'Does your boyfriend know you're here?' or 'We can see you holding hands'. However, when it's hundreds of fans singing the same chant, you suddenly, as a gay man, feel vulnerable and isolated. It re-affirmed the notion that I didn't belong – certainly not there amongst a crowd whose side I was supposed to be on. I felt the same as I had done all that time back on the terraces, in my first game at White Hart Lane.

So when we drew Brighton in the League Cup, we certainly didn't want a repetition of that at our own ground. I staked out the police's Borough Commander, Victor Olisa, before the match. I had worked with Victor when he was in Southwark and his innovative approaches to tackling hate crimes had helped the council win beacon status for community cohesion – people getting on with each other. He responded quickly and assured me that there would be a robust policing plan in operation to deter any name-calling or any offensive chanting.

I wondered at this moment how far the police had come on their journey to accept that such discriminatory behaviour was not on. In the 1970s and 1980s police defended the fact that racists could join the police force, and they did, in droves. Racism wasn't a disciplinary offence as it is now. The argument went that anti-racism was a political ideology and that the police weren't political. One officer, whilst I was a Race Equality advisor, defended the situation to me: "I've got a black Labrador. Now if I want to call it Nigger I should be allowed to. There's nothing wrong with that, but your sort want to stop me." Too right we wanted to stop them, and now, almost thirty years later, I don't even have to answer that paltry argument.

I recall another time when as a students' union official at Warwick University I called on a police officer to investigate the disappearance of a portable music centre, which he called, to my face, the 'wog box'.

It didn't get any better with their response to homophobia. When I returned from university in 1986 I spent one summer night at the cruising ground where I had met Paul from my teenage years. I saw a man threatening and then hitting another man with a baseball bat. Absolutely terrified. I ran back home and plucked up the courage to ring the local police station to report the incident. Rather than take the call seriously, the police officer was more interested in why I was at the woodland. When I retorted that there was an assailant there at that very moment, he simply replied: "Maybe they are getting there just desserts." I slammed the phone down.

These instances in the 1980s really did shock me, because believe it or not, in the 1970s I actually did contemplate a career in the Metropolitan Police. I had entered the 'Young People's Help the Police Competition' in 1975 and received a commended certificate for my entry. I was more that a bit miffed because my brother's submission three years earlier had actually won! He received a trophy and entrance to the national final, which was hosted by the Princess Royal; all I got was a tatty bit of paper. I did get some pleasure from the fact that when I went along to Hornsey Town Hall to be presented with my certificate, it was from my hero, Kenneth Williams from the Carry On films. Chalk and cheese, me and Terry. While I am still wallowing in meeting the comedy actor, Terry was too humble to go his presentation with HRH and when the police came to our door to give him his trophy, he hid indoors while I doorstepped it. I always fancied my myself as some clever clogs in the CID, a bit like Terry Venables' fictional creation Hazell. What put me off the idea was having to do physical education at the training college in Hendon. And to be honest, I probably fancied the actor who played Hazell, Nicholas Ball, rather than actually wanting to be him.

However, there is a much more painful reason why my image of the police changed. It's something that I rarely have spoken about and certainly never written down on paper. It's excruciatingly painful to recall, even now, thirty or more years later. It's something that would have been discounted then by almost anyone I would have turned to for help, and only recently has it become something men feel able to talk about.

It happened on a Saturday night in March 1984 after 'clubbing' in Birmingham city centre. Trying to kill time between closing time at the gay club around 3am and the first train back to university in Coventry at 5am on the so-called milk train, I was loitering. Well, so said the burly plain-clothes police officer who accosted me. He showed me his warrant card and said that I was contravening the 1824 Vagrancy Act, the notorious 'sus law', which had been disproportionately used against black people by the police to harass, intimidate and victimise us. In his view I was loitering with intent to commit a criminal act instead of just waiting for the first train home.

At first I thought it was just something he had said to scare me, so I didn't take it seriously. But then I saw him take money from a young lad who was younger than me and who seemed terrified by his presence. As I protested my innocence he said, "Well it's my word against yours and who do you think they're going to believe?" I was too scared to reply. He went on, "You could of course do something for me that means you won't end up in court". Marching me off to the nearest cash till, he took out all that my card would allow: £25, which was in those days my entire weekly allowance. Sad and shaken, at least I thought this would now be the end of it. Nothing could have been further from the truth. He held me and walked me towards a large set of tower blocks. Then he took me to the top floor and raped me. Yes – forcibly, aggressively and horribly, I was brutally raped. He left me shattered, cold and crying.

I did get the train back, but I didn't get off at Coventry. I went all the way to London Euston and took a night bus home. I cried myself to sleep that day in my bed back at my parents' home, but I didn't divulge what had happened to me, saying only that I had fallen out with my friends. Years later I did tell my Mum, and she was as comforting and lovely as ever. I spoke to a couple of friends at university about it but thought nothing of it until much later in life – delayed shock maybe – but it feels more like a volcano that has been building up in me for many years and one day would break. Male rape was not even a priority for charities then, and there was no befriending or counselling service I could turn to. I suspect many gay men of my generation have undergone similar experiences, unable to get the support they needed.

Later I found out that the West Midlands Police had a terrible reputation for corruption. These were the days before the police had to take tape recordings of statements. One of my gay friends showed me the scars he had after the police in Birmingham had beaten a false confession from him. And of course there's the Birmingham Six, who were falsely accused and convicted of the bombings in the city centre. Their convictions were not finally overturned until 1991, sixteen years after their imprisonment.

Some on the newly-elected Proud Lilywhites committee wanted us to force the club to issue a robust statement before the Brighton encounter, saying that fans would be given stadium bans if they were found to be chanting homophobic abuse. On paper this seemed correct, but it didn't seem proportional to the issue. I thought it would raise the ante and put people's backs up, and so did the Supporters' Trust. After several such statements over the Campbell chant, which was much more blatantly offensive, they thought this was an over-reaction. We decided to back down and put out a simple statement ourselves asking fans to enjoy the match, get behind the team and remember that there would be LGBT people amongst Spurs supporters on the night.

Match day arrived, and as I walked to the ground, I met the Senior Inspector for the night. He assured me that both the police and stewards had been briefed and would stamp down quickly on any such occurrence. The police presence was noticeable and the match was treated in the same vein as when we play West Ham United for example, where supporters were notorious for anti-Semitic chanting. He gave me his mobile number to contact him if anything happened. And that made me uncomfortable, as it I felt a bit like being a teacher's pet. It just wasn't in my DNA to 'grass' on people.

I couldn't relax throughout the whole match. For some reason none of my friends could make the match, so I felt distinctly vulnerable and alone, at a time when I could have done with their support. All the fears that I had suppressed or overcome since the pre-GFSN days came flooding back. Normally at Spurs you do feel apprehensive, because however many goals we score there's always been a feeling that the other team could score one more. This wasn't the reason for my pain tonight. I was like a rabbit in the headlights looking over my shoulder, conscious of any remark someone would make, deciphering every chant. This wasn't what football should be like – I didn't want to be put in this position.

We won 2-0 and there wasn't a whisper of a homophobic chant. Later the police confirmed that there had been no arrests and no reports of a homophobic nature at all. Anecdotal observations by stewards had reported that when some supporters were up for singing such chants, many of them dissuaded them and pointed out the large Proud Lilywhites rainbow flag flying in one of the corners of the stadium. Other members of the Proud Lilywhites were delighted after the match and assumed that the statement that went out on social media had worked. I was just glad that it was all over.

CHAPTER 6

PRIDE AND PASSION

✳

NOVEMBER 2014

The Football Supporters' Federation (FSF) had been approached by GFSN the previous year about celebrating their 25th anniversary with an event called 'Pride in Football', bringing together the growing number of official fan clubs (which they had played a large role in establishing) with the existing membership base of GFSN to create an umbrella organisation to support the sharing of good practice between the two.

However, nothing went quite to that plan. Ironically the LGBT supporters' groups, some of which GFSN helped to set up, were beginning to spawn lives of their own, cutting the umbilical cord from GFSN. Their members were also from a different part of the LGBT community. When GFSN was established in 1989 it was through the auspices of *Gay Times* and appealed to the social instincts of gay men. I can recall no more than five women out of the 300 or so membership. It didn't help that when David and I started to campaign for a name change to include lesbians there was a misogynist backlash, way out of the proposal of simply having a vote on the matter. Although in the subsequent referendum of members we gained a majority, some bright spark said this was a constitutional issue and needed a two-thirds majority. The Spurs supporters drew away from GFSN and both I and David, who was the Social Secretary, resigned from the committee. All these years later, there was still only a handful of women members in the organisation. Enough water had flowed under the bridge for us to be invited back to GFSN for the 10th anniversary in 1999 and it was a poignant moment when the ten original members who were still members, myself included, cut the birthday cake.

From early on GFSN organised an end-of-season social weekend outside the capital, where most of our members lived. It gave us an opportunity to meet other GFSN members from around the country and take in the LGBT scene over the last weekend in May, around the Spring Bank Holiday or the first weekend in June. It got so competitive as to where we would go that we had to put it to a vote of the membership with two or three options for venues. The weekend would start on the Friday night with the option of playing a friendly five-a-side tournament or watching a televised game on Saturday afternoon, with more pub crawling in the evening. Sunday was the formal AGM and a pub quiz. Brighton and Blackpool were favourites with their gay club scenes.

So pubs rather than pitches featured more, until a fully-fledged competitive football tournament took place over the Saturday and Sunday. Slowly but surely that became more important than even the AGM. Soon afterwards, GFSN changed its modus operandi from a social network to one that played competitively on the pitch. By 2002 GFSN had started an 11-a-side national league. It now has 18 teams participating, divided into three tiers, and is still the largest one of its kind in the world. Teams now compete at an international level with on one occasion, Hyde Park in London hosting the Gay World Cup. Over time the supporters' social became dominated by team talk and rivalries between players rather banter between supporters. So a gap developed which the new LGBT supporters groups filled, and crucially, they included more women.

From being a GFSN celebration of its silver jubilee, the agenda of the conference had drifted towards to what the new fan groups wanted, with the organising committee dominated by what are considered the four biggest fan groups: us, the Gay Gooners, the Proud Canaries form Norwich City and Canal Street Blues of Manchester City. So when the event took place near St Paul's Cathedral on a Sunday in the middle of the month, the tension between the new recruits and the old guard of GFSN was simmering. There were rumours that the LGBT fan clubs didn't want GFSN to convene the umbrella group. I could see the merits of both sides of the argument. GFSN was a brand name that had recognition with the authorities – even the Prime Minister, David Cameron, had invited them to a Downing Street reception, after the 2010 election – whilst the new fan groups had, in the main, official backing from their clubs and had appealed across the spectrum of the LGBT community.

In the morning session, we really were proud Proud Lilywhites as the opening address was from Donna Marie-Cullen, the Chief Executive at Spurs. Her speech rejecting homophobia brought back memories of having to endure the abuse we had suffered at the Lane (more of that later) and had Fraser personally writing to Donna after the event, thanking her for her contribution.

There were 80 supporters from 20 teams present, according to the media release put out by Kick it Out after the event. The press were told LGBT fans were united: that couldn't have been further from the truth. Thankfully the media had left by the afternoon and kept to the script provided in that media release. It shows the advantage of telling the press the outcome before an event is over. The organising committee put forward a proposal to establish a Pride in Football network between the fan groups and entirely run by themselves, although it welcomed input, and would work with the existing GFSN. Apparently GFSN representatives had agreed to this before the conference, but when it came to the debate, the worm turned. Passions were running high in the room by now, with some saying that LGBT fans already had a network – the GFSN.

Now if there's one thing I can't stand, it's people saying one thing in private and then doing the opposite in public. For me I addressed the elephant in the room directly: "We all know what this is about. It is about who represents LGBT supporters and how can GFSN say that they can do that when they have so few women members. It's all in the name." Many liked my honesty and many women after the meeting thanked me for my contribution. The vote when it came was a clear, if not totally overwhelming, majority for Pride in Football to be established between the LGBT supporters' groups themselves. However Kevin Miles, the Chief Executive of the FSF, who was chairing the session, was seeking a broad consensus and ruled that the majority wasn't convincing enough. Once again, was this a constitutional matter, I thought, which needed a two-thirds majority.

The day before the conference, we had all been invited to the England match against Slovenia, which was at Wembley. England had had a disastrous World Cup in the summer, losing at the group stage for the first time in over 50 years, but they had kept faith with Roy Hodgson as manager for the EURO 2016 qualifiers, of which this was one. This game wasn't memorable. The first half was dire and it and only just livened up in the second 45 minutes, when the visitors took the lead. Wayne Rooney, in his centenary cap for England, equalised from the penalty spot before Danny Wellbeck scored a brace to give all three points to us.

However, the day was marred for us by some unpleasant behaviour before the game. It shows how much LGBT fans have become used to incidents, because little was said of it later. As we arrived outside the stadium for a photo opportunity, accompanied by Helen Richardson-Walsh, our patron, and her wife Kate, who also plays for England's hockey team, we unfurled our Proud Lilywhites banner along with those from the Canaries, the Gooners and the Blues from Manchester City. As we did so and waited for our photo to be taken, a large burly drunk shouted, "Piss off you fucking queers". Chris, the co-chair from the Lilywhites, shouted back, "Come here and say that!" So there we were with Olympian athletes who had won medals for the country being abused for simply stating who we were outside our own national stadium.

Thankfully we can put this in perspective. There were no further incidents inside the stadium when we displayed our flags, and whilst we were taking photos outside many people gave us the thumbs-up and some even came over to have their photo taken with us.

Maybe though, it was time for a LGBT England supporters group.

Things looked better for Spurs with a 2-1 win at Villa Park followed by the same scoreline away to the Greek side in the Europa League tie. We had a hangover when we returned to the Lane and lost 2-1 to Stoke City. Again it was 2-1 to us away to Hull in the League. We narrowly beat Partizan Belgrade 1-0 at the Lane to go top of our group in the Europa League. November's 2-1 score appeared once more as we beat Everton in the League at home.

CHAPTER 7

FANS FOR DIVERSITY AND FASHANU

✴

FEBRUARY 2015

Spurs got off to a bad start in December with a loss against Chelsea away, followed by a goalless home draw against Crystal Palace. Brighter away from home at Swansea, with a 2-1 win, followed by the same scoreline in a win at home against Burnley and then the same score as we beat Leicester City in the Midlands on Boxing Day. Finally we finished 2014 with a 0-0 draw against Manchester United at the Lane. In the cups, mixed fortunes with a 1-0 loss to Besiktas

*in Turkey in our last group match in the Europa League and
a 4-0 win against Newcastle United in the League Cup.*

*The Premiership new year started with a home win on
the first day against Chelsea, followed by a 2-1 loss at
Crystal Palace. We beat Sunderland 2-1 at home and then
recorded a 3-0 win at the Hawthorns.*

*The FA Cup started with a draw against Burnley at Turf
Moor followed by a 4-2 win in the replay. We went out to
Leicester City in the next round at home 2-1.*

*The League Cup semi-final against League One Sheffield
United was won narrowly on an aggregate score of 3-2 over
two legs.*

For the past decade, February has been designated LGBT
History Month and like Black History Month in October,
and more recently Disability History Month in December,
it is intended to focus on the achievements made by the
LGBT community.

Fans for Diversity was a conference held at the Football
History Museum in Manchester to bring together
supporters who were keen to tackle homophobia in the
game. It was, unlike the earlier Pride in Football event that
season in London, open to all fans and not just those that
were LGBT.

During the conference I met up with the organisers of
Football Supporters Europe (FSE), a group of similar-
minded activists. For me my gay identity is only part of my
character, and essential as LGBT fan groups have been in
challenging homophobia, it is important to link up our
campaign with others, such as making the role of women in
the game more central and standing up to racial intolerance.

The FSE had been launched in 2008 after a Wembley Stadium conference initiated by the Football Supporters' Federation. They had since grown into a member-led organisation with representatives from 48 countries in Europe. Although officially recognised by UEFA, they had kept their independence and often challenged the corporate business-led practices in football. They also believed that LGBT groups should work with other fans in promoting diversity. This got me thinking about the Proud Lilywhites: shouldn't we allow all fans to join as members?

The main speaker and highlight for the media was Thomas Hitzslperger, the ex-German and Aston Villa player who had come out since his retirement. He spoke with much eloquence and thought that we weren't far off from the day when a number of players came out; it was not a question of one or who, but more of when and how many. He also regretted not coming out whilst he was playing and said he now felt wary of being labelled a spokesman for the others who still played.

For me there were two highlights that brought home the international significance of what we were trying to achieve. The first involved a Ugandan refugee from Norway. He said that when Africans viewing at home on TV saw their idol wearing a football against homophobia T-shirt or with the rainbow flag so prominent, it began to raise questions about LGBT rights. The second was Showan Shattak from Sweden, who had been part of their campaign 'Football Fans against homophobia'. Now they hadn't just used the standard rainbow motif on their banners, they had also included a picture of Manchester United's Paul Scholes and Gary Neville kissing each other. This had provoked a reaction that lingered when the same flag was used at a Gay Pride march, when fascists disrupted the procession and targeted Showan, who was left hospitalised after an attack, with a fractured skull.

Football, the world's game, had a responsibility to tackle LGBT inequality, especially in those countries in the world where it was illegal to be gay. This international dimension had also been brought home to me when I had been asked to participate in an international LGBT trades union conference in Brazil in 1994. As a member of Britain's largest public sector union, UNISON, I spent most of the 1990s campaigning for LGBT rights through being a member of their national LGBT members' committee. Brazil had just climbed out of a period of military dictatorship and was making its first tentative steps to democracy in the early 1990s. I met many activists of similar age to me who had spent time imprisoned because they were gay and union members, and some of them had been tortured. It was enough evidence for me to thank my parents for making the decision to leave Kenya, where homosexuality is still illegal, and settle in London in 1968, where it had been only partially decriminalised a year earlier. It reminded me of an online discussion on *The Guardian* website I had undertaken with gay activists in Nairobi, Kenya's capital city. Following that I received desperate messages from gay men who were leading double lives, even getting married to hide their true feelings. I experienced some of that atmosphere during our stay in Rio, as we were routinely followed by the police whenever we ventured outside our hotel venue, once being stopped from entering a bar by armed officers. For once my Brazilian heritage (on my mother's side two generations back) wasn't a favourable card to play. The police weren't convinced I was a true Brit until my passport was shown, and even then I'm sure that only a discreet bribe stopped me being arrested.

Unlike Germany and many other countries in Europe, England doesn't have a tradition of confronting racist and homophobic fans head-on in the way some so-called ultra groups have. There are some outside the professional league; the most notable amongst them are Whitehawk in Brighton; Clapton in Hackney and Dulwich Hamlet in Southwark. Some of these supporters band together and make the terraces into a party rather than a competitive atmosphere, but are just as noisy and boisterous singing anti-racist and anti-homophobic songs. I was pleased to be invited to Dulwich Hamlets from the Ryman League to see this in practice when they played a friendly against the top gay men's team, Stonewall. It was also an opportunity to meet some GFSN members. However, the ones I recognised had long since retired and one was running the line as one of the referee's assistants.

Hitzlsperger isn't the first top-flight footballer to come out. The chant 'He's one of our own' would be gratefully sung by LGBT supporters, if more would come out during their careers. A female footballer, Casey Jones, has come out, and in terms of the men's game, there are players who have come out in lower leagues, both here and abroad. Notably Robbie Rogers, who played for Leeds United, has come out whilst playing for Seattle Sounders, the MLS side, in the United States. Roughly speaking there are 5,000 football professionals in the UK and even given conservative estimates, at least 50 of them will be from the LGBT community. So why does the closet door keep so firmly shut? There are out gay sportsmen in other sports, in the media and amongst the acting fraternity.

For one player however, the closet door did open and it ended up costing him his life. Justin Fashanu was not only the first million-pound black player in the old First Division of the Football League when he was bought by Nottingham Forest in 1988, he was genuinely recognised as one of the greatest black footballers of all time. He had in his last season at Norwich City scored the BBC Goal of the Season, which would forever immortalise his talent. In the era of homophobic hatred of the 1980s where there was still no anti-discrimination laws and only male sex in private with those aged 21 and over was considered legal, Fashanu faced a hostile and unrelenting environment, from the media and the terraces. I don't recall any support been given to him by his peers – in fact many went on the record to say that they wouldn't play football with him.

At around the same time the GFSN had established itself, and we became supporters of Justin by default. I met him at a match at Brentford whilst he was playing for Torquay in February 1992, just before his 31st birthday. He was such a generous, friendly man who always had to time to chat and talk. He was a regular at the Coleherne, at that time London's oldest gay pub and also my local, in Earls Court. We would always nod to each other and at times shared stories. Being out, Christian, black and into football, gave us a common currency and Justin was intrigued with my sexual exploits and glad that he had met someone who was not going to ask too many questions about his.

On one occasion I told him of my trip to Dublin in 1991,

ostensibly on a study tour from work to find out more about travellers' education. I had used my spare time on the trip to visit one of the city's gay saunas, run by a skinhead couple I had met in Mykonos. They told me I would have a cracking time in their establishment, as I had the novelty value of being one of the few Asian skinheads Irish lads would ever meet. In fact they insisted that those who used the sauna were more likely to meet a priest than someone like me.

One story I retold to Justin has now gone into Irish gay folklore. When one priest fainted in the sauna, overcome by a combination of steam and amyl nitrate (more commonly known as 'poppers'), he thought he was dying, and requested the holy sacrament of the last rites. Before long, it's been told, there was a queue of other priests ready to give him the sacrament. Justin took my recommendation and often went to Dublin to relax, and he certainly had no shortage of attention.

The last time I saw him was in April 1998, and he didn't quite look his usual self. He told me that he'd just left the USA, where he had now become a football coach, after allegations were raised against him. He said they were all untrue, but mud sticks. He didn't want to talk further so I said goodbye, not knowing that this would be the last time. Ten days later I learnt the awful news that Justin had taken his own life, by hanging himself near a gay sauna in London. A terrible indictment of the hate-fuelled time, which unfortunately still seems to deter those footballers who may think of coming out today and send them an early warning signal.

Justin was born on the 19th February 1961 and to commemorate this day, the Justin Campaign was established in 2007. It asked football clubs to combat homophobia by holding an event on that day. It had slowly taken root and had grown to the extent that that year a whole month of activities had been planned. It is now known as Football v Homophobia, and most of the clubs with LGBT fan groups had done something. Arsenal produced a campaigning film about homophobia without any player actually mentioning the word – more of that later. Manchester City players wore Football v Homophobia T-shirts before their match whilst warming up, whilst the Proud Canaries had done a lap of honour around the pitch at Carrow Road with their flag.

The Proud Lilywhites asked Kick it Out to designate the Arsenal game as one where we could promote our fan group and leaflet other supporters about our cause. They agreed, and I was joined by David, Fraser and Vince to help hand out leaflets outside the main entrance to the West Stand, where we had a stall. After all these years, and now through the recognition of both the club and Kick it Out, we had been able to promote our message to those attending the big derby match. For our efforts we got a pre-match stadium tour and our photograph taken on the pitch, this time with the Kick it Out flag. The match itself was just as memorable and rounded off the perfect day at the Lane, as we gained our 50th League win against the Gunners. The atmosphere rocked as Harry Kane scored twice – the first was his 21st goal of the season and we won 2-1.

As part of the rebuilding of the stadium, Spurs had already completed the first phase of the project, which was a Sainsbury's megastore with an underground car park and gleaming new offices resplendent in white: Lilywhites

House, which would house the club's staff as well as the new premises of a University Technical College for students taking pre-foundation degrees in sports coaching. As part of the month's activities I had agreed to run a course as part of the students equalities module and was assisted ably by Helen, our patron.

Although most of the participants were black and some were from Christian evangelical backgrounds, like the one Justin had come from, not one person knew of him. By the end of the session and showing how creative and assiduous a player he was, many had been keener to learn about homophobia. I have done similar sessions in sixth form and further education colleges, where there has been a clear gender divide in those interested. Some, not all, boys have associated being gay with femininity, and it is noticeable that when I showed how masculine Justin was and how great a football player he was, the room became more animated and it wasn't just the girls answering all the questions. By the end of the session the consensus seemed to be that whatever one's personal beliefs, the sports field or changing rooms shouldn't be an arena for discrimination. I was really hopeful that this generation, unlike ours, which was never permitted to discuss such issues, would be better all round. The students were really impressed by Helen's bronze medal and Spurs were so pleased that the Community Foundation donated a sum of £1,000 to the Football v Homophobia campaign.

For me the ideal model of Fans for Diversity is at Millwall. Now many of you reading this and mindful of that club's soiled reputation have lost any faith in my football knowledge for making such a statement? But hear me out.

Millwall was the first supporters' group to establish an anti-racist charitable trust, MART, the Millwall Anti-Racist Trust, which is separate from both its Community Scheme and the club itself. Supporters felt they had to take the challenge up themselves to campaign against the tarnished reputation of far-right extremism the fans had obtained over decades. MART has since expanded into 'Millwall for All', and I was delighted to become Southwark Council's officer on the Board at the beginning of 2014. For although the New Den, the club's stadium, is just inside the boundary of the neighbouring borough of Lewisham, it is from Bermondsey and Rotherhithe rather than New Cross that the team's support originates. The Millwall for All Board has representatives from the Pink Lions, the club's LGBT group, and a representative from the Supporters' Trust, and it also has disabled, black and older people. Amongst its advances, it has held football sessions for young boys and girls on some of the impoverished estates in nearby neighbourhoods, disability access surveys, and walking football for older people. This for me is stronger than any LGBT fan group on its own, or even a community anti-racist initiative, it is led by supporters for supporters.

Millwall is also the first club in the country to produce its own promotional film on LGBT issues. It is unique and authentic with a lesbian from the women's team, the Lionesses, featured along with a gay man from the supporters' trust. And crucially it has players such as the club captain speaking about homophobia, Paul Robinson and a black player, Danny Shittu. It is a delight to watch, after hearing nothing from internationally-ranked players about challenging homophobia. So it came as little surprise to me that when Justin's niece narrated a BBC television programme on her uncle, that the only present-day footballers who were willing to participate were from Millwall.

When Millwall reached their first FA Cup semi-final at Wembley Stadium in April 2013, it was my suggestion that the Council should present Paul Robinson with a plaque to mark the occasion and that the team's flag should fly from the Council flagstaff. I thanked Paul personally for his TV appearances and he replied: "But why are you thanking me? We all feel the same."

Top man, first class club, and the supporters deserve more praise.

After that win against Woolwich, we lost a five-goal thriller at Anfield followed with a 2-2 draw against the Hammers, Kane scoring the equalising penalty with the last kick of the game. Little wonder then that he became only the second player in Premiership history to win consecutive Player of the Month accolades.

CHAPTER 8

OUT ON TOUR

✹

FEBRUARY 2015

It was time to take the Proud Lilywhites rainbow flag on tour. We had drawn Fiorentina in the Round of 32, the first knock-out phase of the Europa League. After drawing 1-1 at the Lane in the first leg, the second lag was held in Italy in our last match of the month.

The first time I saw Spurs play Fiorentina was in a pre-season friendly against the Italians at the Lane in 2010. It would be the only game where I denied being gay. A friend who worked for the Foreign Office at the time, Peter, was chaperoning a diplomatic guest from Sudan, where men can be executed simply for being gay. It is a sobering thought that at the time of writing there are still 12 countries in the world where this is the case. When he asked me why I wasn't married, instead of saying that the law wouldn't let me, I simply stuttered that I hadn't met the right woman.

Fiorentina wasn't the first time I had been in Europe following the Spurs with LGBT fans. In the years since Spurs have qualified for the UEFA Cup or Europa League, by bent of winning the League Cup or a top six finishing position in the Premiership, I've managed to visit some historic European cities. I try to spend a few days in the city rather than just travelling on the day for the match and returning the day after.

The first time abroad was with Fraser in 2006, when we played Bayer Leverkusen. We stayed in Cologne and managed to see the players as their bus left for the game. We didn't have tickets for the actual game and were suspicious of buying them from touts. In the end we watched it on television in the hotel on Channel 5. We had come all that way to watch the match on television – well not quite, as it was also Bear Weekend on the gay scene and we spent an inordinate amount of time with furred gay men dressed in leather. One night the bar we went to was full of Spurs fans undeterred by the fact that it was a gay venue. As I overhead one supporter say, "It does good beer and we're on tour, so I couldn't give a toss." On this tour I also met my childhood hero Martin Chivers, who had scored a brilliant goal at Molineux that won us the inaugural UEFA Cup final in 1972.

The following year I went to Seville on my own and I so wish that I had been in a group. It was the quarter finals of the UEFA Cup. Seville stays in the memory, though not for the ambience or the locals but for the brutality of the police, who made baton charges amongst our fans for no other reason than the fact that we claimed we had a penalty. Rather than asking us to be seated, they just hit everyone over the head who was standing and shouting, and you didn't have to be standing, as one wheelchair user found out, because he was battered as well. At half-time we thought we had escaped the melee, only to find the Guardia Civil at the bottom of the stairs in the walkway, laying into people as they went to the toilet. Fortunately I just about escaped a beating, whilst the club lost the match 2-1. It was also supposedly after the match that one or two on the club's Board sounded out the Seville coach Juande Ramos to take over from Martin Jol, which did happen eventually by the time of my next tour.

In 2008 in the first round of the UEFA Cup, we were drawn to play in Poland. I recall Krakow not only for the ability of the Wislaw fans to out-sing us but by the way they swayed in unison for the whole ninety minutes. Krakow is a charming and relatively cheap place to visit and for a good Catholic boy like me, just the place I ought to be touring, as it's the home of the former Pope, now Saint, John Paul II. There had been rumours of potential trouble with right-wing fascists amongst the Polish fans targeting Spurs because of our Jewish connections. When the game ended in a 2-1 win for us, the Polish police weren't taking any chances, and they held us back in the stadium for more than 90 minutes after the match while the home crowd cleared. This incensed some of our supporters and there was a lot of clattering of fences and riot shields before we were escorted back to the city centre.

In our first season in the Champions League in 2010-11, I treated it as if it might be my one and only opportunity to watch Spurs on the biggest stage and in the most famous stadiums in football. The first visit was to see us play in Switzerland in the play-off round against Young Boys of Berne, and neither I nor Fraser could stop laughing as we entered the Wankdorf Stadium to see the young boys play. We soon stopped smiling however, as the Swiss side were 3-0 up before we recovered, and we lost the match 3-2. We stayed in Zürich and travelled to the match in Berne by train. Although expensive, the rail service was very reliable and quick. We were amazed at the number of Swiss Spurs fans. They hadn't started watching us because of Christian Gross or Ramon Vega, but in the main because they had seen Paul Gascoigne and Gary Lineker play for England and associated us with flair and exciting football. We won the second leg of the tie 4-2 and so qualified for the group stage of the competition. At the time of the second leg I was ashamed to think what the Swiss fans must have thought of the public toilets on Tottenham High Road, which are a dilapidated disgrace compared to the perfectly clean urinals in Switzerland.

We were drawn in a tough first round group and we chose a visit to Milan to see Spurs play Internazionale in the San Siro. David joined me for the trip, which is probably the best I have been on. Not for the stadium though, which remains incomplete and a testimony to the lack of public funding. There are no lifts and literally a hole in the ground is all that counts for a toilet for the away fans. However the match itself was, without doubt, the best Spurs away match

I have witnessed. After again going behind, this time to the tune of four goals, a magnificent individual performance and hat-trick from Gareth Bale meant that at the end we celebrated as we would have if we had won. We qualified to meet AC Milan, again in the San Siro for the first leg of the round of 16. I stayed in Verona, visiting Vincenza and Padua. This time we won 1-0 and with a goalless draw in the second leg, we qualified for a mouthwatering tie against Real Madrid in the Bernabeau Stadium. Despite losing 4-0, the stadium, with its museum, was one of the best I have been to.

In 2011-12, we qualified for the UEFA Cup's replacement, the Europa League, and I visited Athens to see us play PAOK Salonika in the first round group. When I arrived in the strike-torn country, although I benefited from everything being cheap, as the Greek economy was collapsing, the down side was that I had to endure a six-hour rail trip, in the midst of a train drivers' strike, to see the match. When there I had to watch our youth side play in a boring 0-0 match. Now there is resting players and there is taking the piss, and I was angry that I had travelled so far for so little. Even the spectacle of seeing topless Greek lads on the other side of the pitch didn't pacify my feelings.

The following season I travelled to the eternal city of Rome for our game against Lazio in the Europa League. There was a particularly poignant moment before the match as Paul Gascoigne, who had joined Lazio after his time at Spurs, did a lap of honour to a standing ovation from both sets of supporters. That was all though that united us, as before the match, Spurs fans in a pub had again been the target of an anti-Semitic attack. The game ended goalless, but I couldn't help feeling for Gazza; he looked frail and he had to be assisted whilst he walked slowly round the pitch. Rome is of course the most romantic city in the world. You can spend hours, days, weeks in the city before seeing all it has to offer. We spent a day at the Vatican. I had been there in 1982 and met the pope from Krakow whom I mentioned earlier. This time I had even a greater surprise, bumping into the Spurs squad and then the manager, Andre Villas Boas, in the Sistine Chapel. Unfortunately this is one area where photos are strictly forbidden so I couldn't take any selfies with the team.

In March 2013 I took my longest trek yet to the northernmost city in Europe, Tromso. I spent a few days in Oslo before travelling by air to see Spurs play in sub-zero temperatures. My dad had always told me that the kindest people he ever met were from Norway and I have to say that I found that to be true on my visit. For example, every time I slipped due to the snow or ice there was always someone who would pick me up and come straight to my assistance. It is the weirdest environment I have ever seen a football match in, with just a couple of hours' daylight every 24 hours. We might have won 2-0 but the Norwegians had won many friends with their hospitality.

Of all the stadiums, Benfica's Stadium of Light, rebuilt for Euro 2004, is the one I found the most comfortable. I first visited Lisbon in 1980 because many of my relatives had sought refuge there from Mozambique and Angola as exiles, following wars of independence against Portuguese rule. When I revisited the city for Euro 2004, the changes since Portugal had joined the European Union were profound. My Goan-descended relatives had fully integrated into

Portuguese society and the capital was now abundant in wealth. The Benfica stadium was part of that renaissance of Lisbon. Now in 2014, Portugal had gone into recession, not as deep as the one I witnessed in Greece, but still unsettling nevertheless. The regenerated areas I had seen just ten years before were now largely empty as many young people had left, ironically some of them to the now booming economies of the former African colonies and to Brazil. The Stadium of Light had now added the obligatory football museum, which I found to be even better than the one at the Bernabeu. It was the Round of 16 and we lost the match 3-1 and then drew the home leg 2-2, going out 5-3 on aggregate.

And so that brings us up to Fiorentina this season. Along with a couple of others from the Proud Lilywhites, we decided to stay in Bologna. What I hadn't checked were the times of the train from there to the match and back. We decided to spend the day of the tie in Florence, so the time of the train out didn't really matter and we calculated that we would just be able to get the last train back to Bologna. Either that or we would have to spend the whole night out. To calm our nerves, we spent the day at the Uffizi gallery. There are so many masterpieces to see that one could easily spend a few days in there.

As we unfurled the banner in the ground we realised that we didn't have anything to tie it to the fencing around the pitch. However, we did take the photo just to provide evidence that we had taken the good fight against homophobia abroad. We lost the match quite convincingly and we were lucky not to lose by a bigger margin than the eventual 2-0 scoreline. We had to run to catch the last train as, as in Switzerland, Italian trains are famous for sticking to the published timetable.

Whilst we were in Bologna, we also made contact with the LGBT group 'Bugs Bologna'. They are a sports-loving and playing group, many of whom study at the famous university in the city. Despite the city being noted for its Communist Mayor, LGBT visibility, like many cities in Italy, isn't as strong as elsewhere in Europe. The debate about same-sex marriage has brought out a reactionary backlash, most notably that led by the Catholic Church. I could understand how they felt, remembering my own Catholic background cemented at school and driven by my devout parents. In my teenage years I went through a phase of believing that becoming a priest would lead me from a life of sin and debauchery of being gay. More realistically however, I thought I could hide my sexual preferences and the inevitable taunts from both family and friends about why I wasn't dating a female or wanting to 'settle down'. I had spent time at a missionaries' retreat in Mill Hill and even befriended a gay priest. I went to weekly prayer and reflection sessions at his vicarage in North London, where there was an ever-increasing circle of gay seminarians struggling between their homosexuality and their faith. One week when I went along, I asked where one of the other regulars was. I learnt from the priest that he had committed suicide the week before, unable to reconcile his sexuality with the teachings of the church, which saw homosexuality as being 'intrinsically disordered.'

I never returned for another session.

CHAPTER 9

CUP FINAL DAY

✳

MARCH 2015

Just a couple of days after playing Fiorentina, we faced our nemesis Chelsea in the aptly-named Capital One Cup. The League Cup, as I have already called it, has had many sponsors down the years from Milk to Worthingtons to Carling and it is now sponsored by a credit company. There is only one team I would hate losing to at Wembley more, and that's the Gooners. Despite the billions poured into Chelsea by Roman Abramovich, we could still say that we had an unbeaten record against the Blues in Cup finals. In 1967, when we first clashed together at the national stadium in the FA Cup Final it was labelled the 'Cockney Cup Final' as it was the first such occasion that two teams from London met at this stage. In preparation for this match I watched that 1967 final again on DVD. We won 2-1 and what really interested me was the commentating from the BBC's Kenneth Wolstenholme. At one stage you can hear supporters booing the other side and he states that this sort of behaviour is creeping into the game and is unacceptable behaviour. It would be less than a decade later that police would have running battles with supporters on and off the pitch, let alone booing.

Of course I was too young, and I wasn't even in the country to see the 1967 final. The first I recall watching was the Chelsea v Leeds United FA Cup final in 1970, which went to two matches; I nearly said two rounds, as it was more of a boxing bout, given the battering each team gave to the other in terms of fouls on the pitch. Mum got wise to the fact that we looked forward to this Saturday in May when the FA Cup final was held and she enforced a rule that we wouldn't be able to watch the match if we didn't go to confession the day before in church. In those days we would have done anything to watch the match, as it was the only live one shown on television in the whole season.

The League Cup final was in March and in its early days, the competition found it difficult to create a perch for itself amongst the football hierarchy. Several First Division clubs didn't enter the tournament until European qualification was given to the winners. Spurs has since won it four times, twice in the 1970s, the first against third division Aston Villa in 1971 and two years later against Norwich City; in between, in 1972, we'd lost a semi-final to

Chelsea. In those days, ITV had exclusive rights to show extended highlights of the match on the day after in their Sunday football programme The Big Match.

Here I should point out that as well as idolising Martin Chivers I also thought Brian Moore, the ITV presenter and commentator, was the bee's knees. I wrote to him once and he actually replied. Moore was a director at Gillingham but he did have a soft spot for both Spurs and West Ham, or at least that's what he told me!

It would be another ten years, 1982, before we appeared in another League Cup Final, this time against the mighty Liverpool. I say 'mighty' because they became the team of the decade, winning numerous League titles and Cup Finals. A tired Spurs succumbed in extra-time to a 3-1 defeat. It would be the first time the club had lost at Wembley, but certainly not the last. Surprisingly, the match still wasn't shown live on TV and like the seventies I had to rely on a radio commentary by another great in my eyes, Bryan Butler on BBC Radio 2. Many a time as Spurs ventured into Europe I listened to his midweek commentaries when I was supposedly tucked up in bed.

We played Leicester City in the League Cup final of 1999 at the old Wembley, which by this time was creaking at the seams. I have to say that over the 90 minutes, this was the worst cup final I have ever seen. It only sprang to life with the sending off of our fullback, Justin Edinburgh, as Robbie Savage simulated a dive. However, we got the final word, with a goal by Allan Nielsen in the last minute of added-on time. It may have been the first League Cup final I had seen but we nearly didn't get to see it at all. We had managed to get 12 tickets, all on the same row, and whilst 10 of my friends went to have a few beers, Vince and I were left alone holding the fort, and just as well, because some fans with duplicate tickets for our exact same seats turned up. Fortunately the stewards decided that possession was nine-tenths of the law and they were ushered away. If we hadn't been there in situ, so to speak, we would have lost all our seats. You can imagine how often Vince and I kept reminding our friends about this. Later we would find out that a couple of staff in the Spurs ticket office had been sacked for fraud. In a way who could blame them, as they had been waiting eight long years, since the 1991 FA Cup Final, for such a chance.

Both the FA Cup and League Cup competitions were moved to the Millennium Stadium in Cardiff whilst Wembley was being rebuilt at the start of the 21st century. In 2002 we reached the final of the League Cup to play Blackburn Rovers, and we were favourites. We were unlucky that day to come across a goalie in top form, as Rovers keeper Brad Friedel played a blinder. I thought it was a bit remiss of Hoddle not to stay on the pitch with the team to get his losers' medal and commiserate with us.

And then to 2008, when we played much better as underdogs in a new Wembley Stadium and after extra time, we beat Chelsea 2-1. More of this later. The following year we made an appearance in the final against Manchester United and again their goalkeeper, Ben Foster, played so well to defy us. He didn't have much to do when the match went to penalties though, as ours were atrocious.

2015's was therefore our eighth Cup Final appearance and our second against Chelsea. It was the first in our enlarged group, the Proud Lilywhites. I could sense some tension between us, the old guard of twelve supporters that had coalesced around me, David, Vince and Fraser and a new vanguard of about six from the Lilywhites Committee. There was an age difference of about fifteen years, we had accommodated straight friends and were all season ticket holders, while they were in the main club members or armchair fans. It's inevitable that when the only common currency is your sexuality, there are bound to be differences. We were all definitely left of centre, whilst the new brood were less politically aware. They also spent an inordinate amount of time on their latest gadgets either texting, posting or tweeting on social media whilst we preferred to actually talk to one another. This, along with how I felt after the Brighton game, began my re-evaluation of my role as co-chair. I was as much to blame, being settled in my ways and the ways of the existing GFSN group. It was time to handover to a new generation, I began to feel. Before the match we donned Harry Kane masks at a kosher restaurant in Baker Street, which is where we usually all meet before travelling up to Wembley. It was a pleasant meal but an unnerving train journey as somehow we got on one full of Chelsea fans, many of whom began hurling anti-Semitic abuse and chanting the usual taunts about gas chambers. Not what you expect from dads in their fifties accompanied by their grandchildren.

The game itself was one with few chances and Chelsea won rather luckily, with two deflected goals for John Terry and Diego Costa. So another record tumbled. When we did inevitably get to play Chelsea in a FA Cup Final, I felt sure my nerves wouldn't be able to survive. Losing to Chelsea in a final is unbearable. I suppose the 5-1 thumping we got from them in the FA Cup semi-final was worse by the scoreline, but this felt just as bad.

I returned to work on the Monday to find that the Council was fearing more cuts from central government if Labour failed to win the General Election in a couple of months' time, so they had offered a blanket voluntary severance policy which meant that anyone could take a redundancy package and leave –you didn't have to be over 55. I was just 50, so it would be madness for me to leave, surely? Remembering that bucket list, I thought what the heck, let's get out of here. So I took up the offer.

Our form in the Premiership improved with a 3-2 win at home against Swansea followed by a 2-1 victory at QPR. We had a setback at Old Trafford though, losing 3-0 before taking all three points in a thrilling end to the month, as we defeated Leicester City 4-3 with Harry Kane scoring a hat-trick.

PART 2

✳

2015/16

CHAPTER 10

NEW BEGINNINGS

✳

MAY 2015

I didn't stand for Chair of the Proud Lilywhites for another season. I didn't go quietly however, and with hindsight, I regret that. I caused a bit of a stink over the Committee's plans to allow for nominations for positions at the AGM itself, as well as before the actual meeting. Now anyone who has run meetings of this type knows this would be bound to create difficulties, as how could people not at the meeting vote for candidates nominated at the AGM, and what if someone stood for a post that already had a candidate nominated? I should have discussed this further with the Committee, but I felt aggrieved. I had been selected by the Committee to run the AGM and now they seemed to be pulling the rug from under me. I complained to the club, which after an investigation did come out on my side. I did feel vindicated and even put in my nomination to re-stand, but even if I had been elected, there were many on the Committee who wouldn't work with me, so I withdrew my candidature and left them to it.

This sad state of events was primarily driven by anger. I have had trouble managing and being appropriate about showing anger and displaying assertiveness, and more importantly knowing the difference between the two. Maybe the volcano of enduring that rape and being reminded by it at the Brighton game earlier this season had finally erupted. It certainly felt like that.

Just before tearing into the Committee about their AGM plans I also heard of the death of a friend. He was an actor, like me in his fifties, who had grown up during a period where he couldn't declare his sexuality openly for fear of it finishing his career. I still can't publicly name him, but things did improve for him and those in the know, so to speak, knew about his sexuality. I would often bump into him prior to matches at the Lane, as Tottenham was his home. On one such occasion Fraser jokingly remarked that he was the campest man he'd seen on Tottenham High Road, not realising that as an actor he was typecast as a villain.

I was eternally grateful to this man, as he introduced me to one of his co-stars in a long-running BBC drama series, and I began to have a fling with him, even though he had a long-term partner himself who was a deputy head teacher. Both of them invited me to their notorious Sunday teatime parties, which often ended in debauchery. I can't say that I participated as I was keener on having the actor for myself. Technically of course such things as gay orgies were against the law, which outlawed homosexual contact between more than two adults, even if it was in a private home. I was glad he was in an open relationship as I could be 'his bit on the side' and we even had weekends together, ironically in Brighton, which is now my home of course.

Then things stopped, and the Sunday teatime parties were suddenly cancelled. A few weeks later it all, as they say 'came out in the wash'. My lover's long-term partner had been outed in the Sunday tabloids, simply because of his role at a primary school. It seems that one of the participants at the parties was slightly younger than 21 and to earn a bit of cash he had gone to the newspapers with stories of vicars and teachers with actors and rent-boys, the sort of thing which tabloid newspapers loved in the Thatcherite period. Added to this was that one of the participants in the party knew the PM, so you had a sex scandal. The fact that the school in question knew their deputy head was gay and that parents, staff and governors gave him a vote of confidence cut no mustard with the press. My lover decided to give up his promising acting career and his partner took early retirement. It dawned on me that anyone, at least in those days, who was gay, was fair game to be thrown to the papers and devoured by the media.

My exit from work was far more amicable. After a couple of weeks grieving over our loss at Wembley, I did ponder on whether I was making the right choice. I had been in paid employment for nearly 30 years and hadn't had to think about paying the bills, as there was always the safety net of the monthly salary going straight into my bank account. I was only just 50 and would have to find another job before I could draw on my pension. Yet when I returned to work, I decided not to withdraw my resignation. It was time for pastures new.

And then in the post came an invitation from Football Supporters Europe (FSE) to attend and speak at their annual conference in Belfast.

As in 2002 and 2008, after playing League Cup finals, our season tailored off in the remaining two months. In April we only won one match 3-1 away at Newcastle. We lost 1-0 at home to Aston Villa and drew 0-0 away to Burnley and 2-2 to Southampton. May saw us lose 1-0 at home to Manchester City and 3-0 away to Stoke. We recovered to win both our last two games – 2-0 at home to Hull City and 1-0 away to Everton.

So we finished 5th and won a place in the Europa League. Harry Kane won both the PFA Player and Young Player of the season awards, scoring 21 goals in the Premiership alone.

CHAPTER 11

BELFAST, BLANCHFLOWER AND GAZZA'S TEARS

✳

JULY 2015

Arriving in Belfast at the suitably named George Best Airport, I was very fortunate to get a luxury limousine to the college campus where the conference was being held. I had been invited by the organisers to chair, or as they now say in EU parlance, moderate, a discussion on homophobia and discrimination in the beautiful game. Back to the car – the grant the FSE receives from UEFA hardly stretches to a Morris Minor, let alone a limousine. I was extremely lucky to hail the first taxi available, which just happened to be a limousine.

In Northern Ireland, given the history of the troubled province, it suddenly dawned on me that I needed to be politically sensitive. I can be quite an outspoken bloke at the best of times and always have a tendency, when arriving in a new foreign city, to ask the cab driver from the airport three things: Does he support a football team; If so, has he heard of the Spurs; and what does he think of the current Prime Minister in his own country (not ours, as Thatcher, Blair and Cameron have more than likely rubbed up his country in some bad way). As always, football and politics.

So here goes. "Smart car. Hope you won't be charging extra". It doesn't quite break the ice but I get a polite response: "It's my manager's car, mine broke down earlier today." I avoid politics and yes he is into football, a Manchester United supporter, and as I will find out, so are half the province. The other half, so it seems, are Liverpool fans. At least they can agree on the colour red. And that's the nub of starting any conversation in Northern Ireland – you have to be careful not to take sides. Certainly there will be no conversations started with 'I like Celtic and the time I went to see Spurs play Rangers in a pre-season match was more akin to the Royal Tournament than watching a game.'

The last time I was in Ulster, in 2001, I was routinely assumed to be a soldier. If you know me, you'll laugh out loud at that. However, don't doubt me, there were some pubs I was told to stay out of. Now, fifteen years later, I am a much more portly gentleman, and that may no longer happen. In Belfast, first appearances count for as much as the postcode where you live. Even using the term 'the North' could be provocative to some. Does that mean you believe in a united Ireland and that Northern Ireland isn't, or more correctly shouldn't be, part of the British mainland but is part of the island of Ireland? There are two nations, Northern Ireland and the Republic of Ireland, and what distinguishes this part of the United Kingdom from others is that a significant part of the population in Belfast and the whole of the six counties want to be part of another nation. That's as if significant parts of Northumbria for example, wanted to get back to their Viking ancestry and be part of Denmark.

I had arrived in the middle of the marching season, so every corner was emblazoned by a Union Jack or in some cases the Northern Ireland flag, a flag portraying the Queen or one of the local Orangemen's order. This led to some hilarity amongst some of the football supporters attending the Conference, who either thought it was another Jubilee celebration or that we were there during a flag makers' convention. In Ulster however, you don't make jokes about flags, even when one household quite close to the ground we were visiting on the first night, had the Star of David emblazoned on a pole in its front garden. Despite receiving a history tour the following day, many of the conference participants were still none the wiser to the significance of these emblems.

The first night was spent watching my first game of the season. And there's another first. I don't think in all the years of following Spurs and going to the odd neutral game that I have started a football season at the beginning of July. The reason for the match was that it was a qualifying tie for the Europa League. Ah, I can hear the sighs even as I write these words, what is the point of the Europa League? You might well ask. Some Spurs fans think that it's been nothing but trouble. Last season we lost so many games on the Sunday in the League after playing the Thursday in Europe. The tournament diverts half your squad and a considerable number of the first team, thousands of miles away to the outer reaches of Europe, to places even the EU hasn't conquered yet. Spurs fans, including myself, will have gone through all the reasons why the competition is good to be in: it means the first taste of European trips after years of mid-table mediocrity where the squad even failed in the preliminary round of the absurd Inter Toto Cup, which actually was staged in July. Clearly however in the last couple of seasons, it has left us punch drunk and we struggle to play and beat any team we come up against after a Thursday night match, home or away.

Yet here was I about to watch Glentoran, only a short distance from the teachers' college that was our base for the conference. As I came to buy a programme, the seller saw my Spurs pin badge and said he was a keen Tottenham fan himself. I was to find out later, when we were chaperoned by club officials the following day, that he was Danny Blanchflower's cousin's son, or more exactly first cousin once removed. I had touched hands, bought a football programme, spoke to, a descendant of probably the best player ever to have put on a Lilywhites shirt. And just for the anoraks out there (I promise that's the last time I will use that word, not even a raincoat or a duffel coat will ever be mentioned again), Glentoran lost 4-1. Rather unluckily, I thought.

On our return journey after the match, we went a different route and lo and behold amongst all these flags was a row of Rainbow flags – the sign of a gay pub in the heart of what must have been the High Street. Well how nice was that. On enquiring, I was told that the pub had a mixed clientèle, both gay and straight, and no record of harassment and abuse against it. That was really uplifting I thought, because 15 years ago when I had first visited the city, there was little evidence of an 'out' gay scene in Belfast. However, further down the road we passed a Confederate flag, an emblem of the slave-owning southern states in the USA. With one quick glance, all my goodwill for the city had evaporated. Upon waking the next morning I was still troubled by that flag. One can have discussions about the need to display flags of historical and cultural importance, but here was the emblem of slavery, of overt and ugly racism. The flag, I gathered, had been put there by racists to antagonise a young black footballer who played for the juniors in the local team. There was a storm of criticism for the police, who had failed to take the flag down, and many plaudits for those fellow players who took it down and apologised to the young person it was aimed at. I was to find out that racist incidents had mushroomed in the past two decades since the Good Friday Agreement, almost as if another minority was being picked on by the bullies in the playground.

I made my first mistake by asking for a 'Full Irish' at breakfast, when of course what was on offer was a 'Full Ulster', as I was gently reminded. Since the peace agreement, everyone seems to want Northern Ireland to succeed, for businesses and visitors alike. One of the major tourist attractions is the Titanic Museum in a regenerated part of Belfast near the old docks in which the Harland and Wolff shipbuilders still survives today. To my delight I had time spare before the session I was chairing (sorry moderating) to visit this area, and fortune smiled on me as our event coincided with the Tall Ships event. So the harbour was a blaze of activity. The Titanic Exhibition doesn't disappoint. The museum is certainly one of the best I have visited and deserves all the plaudits it has received.

In fact I took so much time visiting the exhibition that I was almost late in returning to the conference for my session. I sat down in front of 100 football fans from 20 different countries and didn't even know the names of the people on both sides of me who I was about to introduce. And they expected me to say a few words. Then a text from my brother, a fellow England fan: "It's 25 years ago today that Gazza cried in Turin." And then it all comes back to me and suddenly I know what to say.

There was I, back in 1990, doomed to watch England humiliated again to a supposedly lesser team in a World Cup, not unlike Morocco four years previously when Ray Wilkins was sent off and Brian Robson injured. It was happening all over again. This time in Italia 90 it is Cameroon's time to punish us. I switch off the television at 2-1 down. Better off not watching at all, I say to myself. Spend the time thinking of better days watching England. Really? Then it all comes back to me, like falling into a deep chasm of perpetual misery.

Germany in 1970 was my introduction to supporting England. We were two nil up and coasting, beating the Germans yet again after 1966 at Wembley, with two goals from Spurs players to boot, Alan Mullery and Martin Peters. At the end we lost 3-2 as Chelsea's Peter Bonnetti was all at sea in the England goal. I got a smack from Terry, my Chelsea-loving brother, when as a six-year-old I made the innocent, yet intelligent, comment that if it wasn't for Chelsea, Spurs would have put England through to the semi-final, where we would have beaten Italy and then been in another final.

Yet worse was to come with Poland in a qualifier in 1973, and another clown of a goalkeeper, this time on the opposition; then Brooking and Keegan missing sitters in 1982 and Maradona scoring with his hand in 1986. It's just not worth the grief. I shall do something else. If England want to throw away their best chance in a World Cup tournament since winning in 1966, by losing to Cameroon, then so be it. After all they did beat the holders, Argentina, in the opening match. We'll be able to survive the humiliation, there's always next time. Who am I trying to kid?

So to keep me occupied, I turn to my other failing interest at the moment: the Labour Party and the next agenda of the Acton Green Branch meeting. Why did I ever volunteer to do this? I haven't got a typewriter, and I've had to borrow one from another member. Let's see now, the next meeting is on the day of the semi-final. Well good, at least I won't have to watch that.

Then from the neighbours I hear a muffled roar. I switch the telly back on and I can't quite believe it – Gary Lineker of Spurs has just scored his second penalty of the match and we've won 3-2, the reverse of 1970, and yet again Spurs have saved England from humiliation and the ritual denunciation of the tabloids. We are through to a semi-final! And on the same night as the Labour Party meeting. Well who cares, perhaps if I don't watch it, then we'll win. Yes, that's it! I'm the bogeyman – if I don't watch, England will win. I stopped watching after that Morocco game in 1986 and we went onto win the next two matches before I was tempted out of hibernation, only to see us lose to Argentina and that flaming cheat Maradona. It won't happen this time. Definitely not.

And so the night of that match in Turin comes around. Looking back, it's difficult not to emphasise the meteoric changes that night would bring to football. Scarred by the three tragedies of Heysel, Hillsborough and Bradford, English football had reached the end of the road; there was nowhere lower it could go. To be honest, I had stopped going to my beloved Spurs, not simply because I was scared off by hooliganism but because I had come back from university a more open and determined individual – open to the fact that I was gay and determined that I wouldn't let the homophobic and racist comments go over my head any more. Also, who did I have to go with?

So the night of the semi-final against the Germans begins and I avoid all contact with the TV ; no Nessun Dorma for me, just a Labour Party discussion instead followed by a few beers later in the West London Trades Union Club, when it will all be over. But what if the meeting is inquorate? Then I'll be forced to see the game! No fears. I walk into the hall and the meeting's quite full, but there seems to be something different. Not one other bloke except for the Chairman turns up and I tell you what, I've never been to a more cordial and productive meeting. No mention of football, no whispers about the score and I actually enjoy myself.

So let's pop downstairs to the club, the match will be over by now and at least I won't have to endure the agony. Yet the England God (or is that Devil?) has one more twist in the tail for me. The match has gone to extra time, it's 2-2 and by all accounts England have been well worth watching. The rest as they say is history, as we lose on penalties.

However, seeing your best player, Paul Gascoigne, also a Spurs legend, engulfed in tears during and after the match softens the blow. Maybe there is a heart to the lion of the English game; maybe it's all right for men to show emotion. It remains a watershed moment in football history (pun intended). Crumbs, it even led to a West End play, 'An Evening with Gary Lineker', and a full-blown film, 'One Night in Turin'. For me and plenty of others in the gay community, it showed a more amenable side of the English game. Maybe, just maybe, the game could get over its image of far-right extremism and violence, and what better way to challenge that old order then being out on the terraces?

That was it. By texting me, my brother had just located the modus operandi for what I should say. 25 years later I am privileged to be in a hall asked to lead a discussion on homophobia in football with supporters from all over the continent. Yet 25 years before, if I'd uttered the words 'gay' and 'football' in the same sentence, people would have asked what on earth I was talking about. Gazza's tears were more than just an expression of emotion. They were very real for those of us who had lost faith in the game we loved. They gave a small opening into discussions about masculinity, pride and what it meant to be a supporter. It was an olive branch that still resonates today.

Unfortunately Thomas Hitzslperger wasn't able to attend, but in his place Ralph Guernicsh, who played for St Pauli in the second tier of the German Bundesliga, joined me. Alongside him was a representative from the Swedish LGBT fan group movement, Asa Wendin, plus Kyle Knight from Human Rights Watch and Kadir Keleq, representing a gay Turkish referee who had received demotion and a lot more trouble for himself since he came out. I was disgusted that our own government had failed to give the referee a visa to attend. It was heartening to hear of straight allies like Ralph, who thought it would be great if more players came out, and about the blossoming of LGBT supporters' groups in Sweden, but it was disheartening to hear of the reaction to the plight of the referee in Turkey. On that same weekend, as we met comfortably in our college venue discussing the pros and cons of coming out, participants in the Gay Pride march in Istanbul had been hosed down with water cannons and bludgeoned with truncheons. Still so much to be done, but it was gratifying that even in the time I had been there in Northern Ireland, I had seen glimmers of hope of what we could achieve if we were strong in solidarity against the cancer of discrimination.

CHAPTER 12

MUNICH, BALE AND THE Y WORD

✳

AUGUST 2015

There was a time when the football season began without much fanfare. You would receive the pools coupon in the post and you'd notice that Australian Football had been replaced with the start of the Football League. If you were lucky you would also purchase one of the football annuals – dads would go for the Rothmans' Yearbook (now sponsored by Sky Sports) and their teenagers would purchase the *News of the World Football Annual* (now attributed to the Nationwide) and quickly go to the last section of both, where all the fixtures would be provided. This was before the advent of the Premiership, Sky pay-for-view television and the internet. Now fixtures are routinely changed for the convenience of those paying to watch in their armchairs. Maybe Brian Clough was right when he said that televised football would be the death knell of the game.

Another change to the game has been the worldwide attention the Premiership clubs have with followers all over the globe, now able to watch games live. Supporters aren't just those at the ground. The Asian and American markets gather followers by the millions, generating a ripe overseas market for merchandise. This gives a growing appetite for the match to travel to where these followers live so they can taste a bit of live football for themselves. Most familiar is the advent of the football pre-season tournaments with clubs travelling to the Far East, North America and Australia for warm-up matches.

I was off to Munich to travel for the Audi Cup, a four-sided tournament with Bayern Munich the hosts playing alongside Real Madrid and AC Milan. This is as close to the season as pre-season matches can get, with only a week left to the start of the Premiership. I was a bit baffled then as to why Spurs was invited, and then I realised that we were the fifth choice – the top four all chose to stay at home. Anyway Munich was a place I also wanted to visit and many have reckoned that the Allianz Arena, where the matches would be played, is the best stadium in the world.

For me it was essential that I take in a visit to the 1972 Olympic Stadium, which Bayern Munich used to call home. It brought back vivid memories of watching the Games in colour and of gold-winning performances such as the one from Northern Ireland's Mary Peters in the pentathlon.

However, it also brought back some very bad memories for me and for all who were there and watching on TV: the shocking deaths of 13 Israeli hostages who had been kidnapped at the athletes' village. Yet the stadium now was a ghost of its former self. The iconic images of the futuristic nets which covered some of the stadium were bleak and daunting. There was no guided tour available when I visited and only a few tatty display boards telling the story. For me it meant that I had now visited six Olympic stadia; Munich is added to those in Los Angeles, Barcelona, Athens, Helsinki and Rome and in many respects this was the bleakest. Yet it was the first Olympics I remember watching on TV. Some sort of memorial for the tragic loss of life wouldn't have gone amiss.

It also brought back painful images for me personally. At the height of the games, my family and I had visited Bournemouth for our annual summer holiday week by the seaside. We had such a lovely time the year before in Eastbourne and we were really looking forward to the week by the Dorset coast (it was Hampshire until the boundary changes of that year). Yet something was wrong from the moment we arrived. Firstly our guest house was located in neighbouring Boscombe, not in Bournemouth itself, and when we got there, even as an eight-year-old, I could sense an unwelcoming vibe in the air. The proprietors weren't that friendly and I soon gathered they hadn't realised when we booked that a group of six Asians would be turning up. Anyway we made the best of what we could, until the last day. It still sends a chill wind through my Mum, Terry and me when we discuss it.

Returning to the guest house after a visit to Chichester,

my brother and I discovered that plastered on the walls of our family room were disgusting signs saying 'Go home Pakis' taken from newspaper cuttings, which were full of stories of Ugandan Asians – British passport-holders who were refugees in Britain after fleeing Idi Amin's dictatorial rule of the African country. Luckily my brother and I saw the racist posters first and only my Mum was told about it. It would have deeply affected my troubled father, who had suffered a severe breakdown two years earlier, and my grandmother, who had only just arrived in the country, if they had witnessed the scene for themselves. We decided not to complain, as we were leaving the next morning. It was one of those shocking instances of direct, in your face racism that we had to endure in the 1970s, and it left me with an indelible scar associated with the 1972 Olympics.

The Allianz Arena however wasn't as disappointing as the Olympic Stadium. It was truly magnificent, rising like the alien spaceship out of the science-fiction film *Close Encounters of the Third Kind,* and it seemed to have been made in another dimension. Inside, the views were no less appealing, and having purchased a seat right at the back of one of the stands, I could see clearly all four corners of the pitch. A magnificent site to behold, yet a poor game to witness. Real Madrid treat Spurs as their B team. It seems that we nurture the players and then sell them to the Spanish side to blossom, in a reversal of what we do to West Ham United. That's not entirely fair. We did see some pretty good years from both of their recent Tottenham acquisitions, Luka Modric and Gareth Bale, but too few seasons to mention. Bale was one of those few players during my time as a season ticket holder who left us breathless for the sheer audacity of his profound talent. And to think that when we first bought him and he played as a full-back I wanted to sell him. What do I know?

If you go back to just before my first season and the reason I paid for a season ticket the following year, a certain Paul Gascoigne comes to mind. He was like Bale, the best player on the planet in 1990-91. After taking England by the scruff of its midfield neck and leading the country to the World Cup semi-finals in Italia '90, he continued in that way at White Hart Lane the following season. By being our top scorer in the FA Cup competition that season, he took the club to its first Wembley semi-final against our arch rivals from Arsenal, and the rest, as they say, is history. Certainly he scored the best goal I have seen from a Spurs player in that match. Despite him having to leave the pitch with a serious injury in the subsequent cup final against Clough's Nottingham Forest, we won against all the odds after extra time.

Four years later and after the next World Cup final, I had mixed views when Jurgen Klinsmann joined us. He was known for his prolific diving in the penalty area, and I was less than convinced that he would make the grade in the rough and tumble of the English premiership. How wrong was I – again! Klinsmann won the fans' hearts by his and the team's thrilling display in the first game of the season at Sheffield Wednesday, this time a 4-3 scoreline in our favour and the best first game of the season I have witnessed. Jurgen and Teddy Sheringham, along with Darren Anderton, Nick Barmby and World Cup Romanian buys Ilie Dimitrescu and Nico Popescu, certainly made us an exciting side to watch. Despite a change of manager and an initial FA Cup ban, we managed to go all the way to the semi-finals that year, 1995, though ultimately we failed badly to recapture the glory of four years previously.

In 1999 we reached our first final in eight years, the penultimate League Cup final played at Wembley Stadium before its redevelopment. The season up to the match will be remembered for one player: David Ginola. We bought the player for a couple of million, loose change then, and he paid us back in buckets that year. His swashbuckling style and galloping runs made him a firm favourite as we nearly made it to another FA Cup Final that year only to lose in the semis once again.

Last season saw Harry Kane raise the spirits with a record amount of goals in a Premier League season for a Spurs player. Again what do I know, as I was convinced, when I first saw him, that Kane, pardon the pun, wasn't Able to meet the demands of the Premiership. How wrong was I for the third time and gratefully so, because if it hadn't been for his combative style, his pace and the sheer knack of being in the right place at the right time to score, we would have had a fairly average season.

As if fate already had it written, it was Bale who would score the first goal against us in the friendly match we played in Munich, with a sublime shot which the keeper should have parried. Not a lot stays in the memory for the remaining 89 minutes of that match except one thing – a raw 19-year-old nutmegging Modric, our own Dele Alli bought from League One's MK Dons for £5 million. Could he blossom into a Gazza, Ginola, Klinsmann, Kane or Bale, I wonder? Time will tell.

Near Munich and on the itinerary of visitors is the

Dachau concentration camp, a bleak reminder of the worst humanity can do. I didn't pay a visit. I had already been to Auschwitz (during the trip I took to Krakow during that Europa League game in 2008), and there seems something ghoulish in going to death camps as if they were Olympic stadia. It's difficult to explain how a visit of this magnitude affects you. You're in a place where hundreds of thousands of people were put to their deaths after being dehumanised, brutalised and tortured. The first thing that gripped me was the silence of the place. No birds sang; the breeze of a cold autumn day was the only noise that rustled the trees. The sheer scale of the brutality is astounding; the Nazis documented every person down to their hair colour. They routinely treated the prisoners as if they were cattle ready for slaughter. Everyone thinking of turning their back on today's refugees or spreading sadistic lies about Jewish conspiracies ought to be made to visit one of these death camps. As we say at Spurs, 'know your history'. A grim reminder of the brutality anti-Semitism can lead to. Not forgetting for one moment the other tortured souls that died there – political prisoners, disabled people, gypsies and travellers, gays and lesbians.

A few years later we all were pressed to take sides in an anti-Semitism debate that engulfed the club. Tottenham Hotspur, like most clubs in North London, including Arsenal and West Ham, have had a history of a significant and visible Jewish following. The only time it becomes an issue is when an opposing club's followers shout anti-Semitic chants, mainly, but not exclusively, by imitating the sound of those now turned-off gas chambers in places like Dachau and Auschwitz. They have also chanted 'Yiddos' at us, after

Alf Garnett used the term in the BBC sitcom *Till Death do us Part*. Ironically the actor who played the oafish West Ham supporter was Warren Mitchell, Jewish himself and a mad Spurs fan.

If this is meant to scare our supporters, it has only done the opposite. It angers us, and more recently we have shouted the Y word, "Yid Army", as a sign of our own aggression. We have, as many commentators have said, including those from the Jewish community, reclaimed the word, just as black people have reclaimed the N word and gay men the word 'queer'. This has been called a defence mechanism to suggest that we are really proud of our Jewish heritage and associations.

I can't quite remember when we first started using the term 'Yid Army'. I think it was more recent than some have suggested. I don't recall it being used, certainly not at matches I attended, until as late as the 1992-93 season. This was when in another FA Cup run to a loss in the semi-finals (Arsenal exacting revenge at Wembley), we played Manchester City at the old Maine Road Stadium in the 6th round. City expected to win and exact their own revenge for us beating them in the 1981 final, in which Ricky Villa scored that memorable goal. How wide from the mark were they that day? In increasingly tense and agitated conditions, a Spurs team stormed through 4-2, and it could have been worse for City if a deliberately missed penalty from Teddy Sheringham had been scored. It was the beginning of the decline of the Blues to the lower reaches of the league in the 1990s. City fans threw everything at us – not on the pitch, but in the ground. Bottles, saliva and insults, including that gas chamber slur, rained down on us. It was then that I heard for the first time a Yid Army song coming back. The match was nearly abandoned due to a pitch invasion by the home fans and we were kept in the ground for our own safety. So that's where I think the Y chant from Spurs fans began. However, there was little debate on the matter, hate crimes were still on a wish list, television commentators were more concerned about the pitch invasion and certainly the FA did fuck all about anti-Semitic chanting.

In 2012 the Society of Black Lawyers created a stir after Spurs fans were heard chanting 'Yid Army' and other more dubious remarks against Sol Campbell, who at that time was playing out the fag-end of his stunted career at Portsmouth. CCTV could capture the culprits and certainly the anti-Campbell song, which I had complained about a number of years earlier in the Spurs fanzine, was racist and homophobic. Spurred on by Chelsea Jewish fan David Baddiel, the club were asked to ban the Y word chant. Battered and bruised – sometimes literally – by anti-Semitic chanting by Chelsea and Hammers fans in particular, which Baddiel conveniently forgot, I wrote to Donald Herbert, Chair of the Society of Black Lawyers and a friend of mine from my days on the National Assembly Against Racism in the 1990s, claiming that the context in which the chant was sung was important considering that we had many Jewish fans who didn't mind the chant and some of whom gloried in its reclamation, and saying that it was daft to call us racists and ask for us to be prosecuted under the now, very new, Hate Crimes legislation. After many debates, even a survey by the club and failed prosecutions, the debate seems to have faded from attention. Not mine though.

I'm not Jewish, so what right, even as a Spurs fan

listening to anti-Semitic taunts, do I have to reclaim the word? I asked some of the Jewish supporters around me where I sit at every home game what they thought. Most of them said they weren't offended by us singing the song as they could clearly see our context, but, and this is a crucial but, they wouldn't sing it, as they knew the pain and suffering it brought to their forefathers when heard in the context of Nazi storm troopers.

This got me thinking, and I believe I saw the light (if one ever does have a eureka moment), when we played Benfica in the last 32 of the Europa League in 2014. I heard the menacing chant of the Yid Army and witnessed how frightened some of the young Portuguese children felt when they heard this as the Spurs contingent were marching to the ground. They hadn't a clue about the intricacies of the debate raging in Britain. And then it dawned on me. Do football supporters ever have the right to call themselves an army? Doesn't it provide an atmosphere of tension? On the first, no, probably not, and on the second, a firm yes. I think everyone in football knows why we sung the Y chant. If everyone does take action when anti-Semitic remarks are made against us, then why is there a need to sing the song? It may have been reclaimed, but now it just inspires aggression and it's time we moved on.

More than time.

In the league, our start was stuttering to say the least. Following a narrow loss to the Red Devils at Old Trafford in the opening game, we had three draws on the bounce against Stoke 2-2, Leicester 1-1 and Everton 0-0.

CHAPTER 13

FEELING QUEER AT FIFA

✳

SEPTEMBER 2015

Zürich is rather an odd city in a peculiar country. Not that that is a bad thing. It has a remarkably well-preserved old town amongst a sprawling modern financial hub. It is the home of FIFA, whose authority for being the guardians of football was daily collapsing. As if the sinking ship of FIFA seemed to be floating merrily away without recourse to any sense of direction, it had finally succumbed to the growing evidence that LGBT football fans – Qatar and maybe Russia World Cups excepted – do exist, for the international HQ in Switzerland played host to the 17th Biennial meeting of

Europe's 'Queer Football Fans' (QFF). Mainly made up of clubs in the German Bundesliga and also with some in Scandinavia and the low countries, QFF represents 35 fan clubs on the continent. I had been invited along by Sven Kitzner, one of their Executive Members, who I had met at the FSE meeting in Belfast, with the aim of moderating a session on international links.

Before the meeting got under way, in the auspicious venue of FIFA HQ, we were taken on an LGBT tour of the city and reminded of the brutality of Nazi Germany. Not content with anti-Semitism, the regime also didn't tolerate any form of 'sexual deviancy' as it termed it and being LGBT in wartime Germany led many to the same concentration camps that the Jewish population were banished to. Yet Zürich was known for its liberal attitude and Switzerland was officially neutral during the conflict. Many flocked to the bars and clubs of the Swiss city where some could be relatively 'out' and live a bohemian lifestyle. Zürich had also earlier played host to Lenin, who lived in the city; from here he had scampered off to his native Russia to lead the Bolshevik revolution in 1917.

Two of the queer football fan clubs are based in Zürich, that of Grasshoppers and Zürich FC, the latter of which played host to our first gathering in their club shop. Both teams share the same stadium, something that thankfully would be unheard of in North London. This is not by choice and owes much to the peculiarity of Switzerland's political system. For a country that boasts the international headquarters of the game's greatest sport and played host to the World Cup finals in 1954, this isn't by any stretch of the imagination a football-friendly country. For the game originated in the public schooling system of the nation, hence clubs like the Young Boys of Berne, and football was not seen as a working man's or for that matter a woman's sport until the middle of the last century. So when the two clubs wanted to build separate football stadiums they came a cropper, due to the Swiss obsession with holding referendums on almost all issues. Simply put, the residents of Zürich, when they have been asked, have not voted to build football stadiums. In a nation with fresh air, mountain glaciers and lots of snow, participation sports such as ice hockey and skiing have remained firm favourites, so both Zürich clubs have to make do with using an athletics stadium. The venue of the Weltklasse plays home to both football teams. To make matters worse for the football pride of Zürich, the stadium reaches its capacity when the Diamond League of Track and Field athletes visit, but even for the local derby between the two football sides, it is never full.

Yet it is in this football-impoverished city that football has its Swiss centre, and what a centre. I had heard stories of the exuberant refurbishments that FIFA had spent money on, but nothing quite matches the descriptions of the place to when you see it in person. Firstly, the headquarters is located in its own park in the city and on entering you feel that you have entered the United Nations, as every flag of FIFA's 200 or so member countries is on display. Each of the seminar rooms is named after football-related matters, like Goal and Referee.

In the morning the session on international links looked at the real problems of holding FIFA World Cups in countries that didn't have a good record on LGBT rights, to put it mildly. Both Qatar and Russia had anti-LGBT legislation in force. There was a consensus that we must campaign for FIFA to guarantee the rights and freedoms of all those attending and that for future tournaments, countries who did discriminate, shouldn't be allowed to bid to hold the tournament.

We were fortunate enough to be taken on a tour of the building after a salubrious lunch and saw the three chambers, which were palaces in their own right. The first was the press conference room, which was unlike any I have seen. Spending the millions that FIFA devours, I suppose the architects felt that an impressive room for the hordes of angry media might pacify the natives. Then onto the chamber where the elected Executive Committee deliberate, which for no particular reason is adorned with a palatial chandelier to match any found in a state ballroom. This is where I lost the translator of our German tour guide, but there were audible whoops of derision when the cost of the diamond crystals that make up the chandelier was announced. Grafted into the elaborate stonework of the walls of the chamber were the names and faces of FIFA's presidents, not that many as most try and stay until they are octogenarians.

Nothing however quite prepares you for what is termed the meditation room (using the word 'prayer' obviously offends atheists). It is a cubed room, cut, we were told, from the finest quartz crystal available on the entire planet. I joke not; as I asked for the description to be translated several times, before closing my gaping mouth, I was told the crystal had been shipped in from Afghanistan and hand-crafted into the magnificent imperial style now on display.

One can see why revolutionaries burn buildings after witnessing the craven splendour and disregard for money the FIFA HQ has.

Lenin should be regenerated to finish off the Czarists still in his former bolt-hole.

The visit gave me time to reflect on why being 'queer' and also a 'football fan' is something to shout about. I would think that most football supporters don't think sexuality is an issue at matches. Why bring your personal matters into the ground, I can hear them say? Yet I would retort, why do some bring their blatant, and at times ruthless, homophobia into the grounds? Some of the things I have had to witness and endure are things no one should be allowed to experience, let alone expected to tolerate. I don't mean just the words slung at players and other fans, such as 'puff', 'tart', 'queer', 'batty boy', 'arse-bandit', all words I've heard fans shout at players and officials in grounds. Maybe things are getting better in terms of racism, but sexism and homophobia are still the poor relations. The number of black and Asian and other ethnic minorities (BAME) watching games, according to the Premiership survey of fans, has increased to about 12% of football spectators, almost the national level for the BAME community in the UK. However it is a scandal that many LGBT fans have to stay in the closet to watch a match, careful not to come out and wary of the scorn not just of opposing fans but of those around them. How many are able to hold hands with their partners? Lesbians have to face the sexism of a still largely male environment and when one of the officials is female, if they make what fans think is a wrong decision, the derogatory comments they have to endure are appalling.

It is a common assumption that football fans only start being offensive if they have had too much to drink. Inhibitions drop, the beer starts flowing and it's just like the old days. Not true however, when it comes to homophobia. One of my worst experiences was at home with fellow season ticket holders who were screaming and shouting abuse against one player, a footballer who isn't even gay, even if that's a pre-requisite, but has had to endure the type of bullying, harassment and abuse that wouldn't be tolerated in any other workplace. For that is what a football stadium is during a match – a workplace for the 22 players, the team officials and the referee and assistants. Would you shout across a crowded office homophobic words against a colleague from another firm?

Yet it was tolerated on our pitch and on our terraces when it came to Graeme Le Saux. He played as a fullback for Chelsea and on one night in May 1999 the abuse around us went through the roof. It was a League match and it came after a notorious homophobic incident against Le Saux in Chelsea's preceding home match against Liverpool, which I will cover later. In our match no stewards acted, no one reproached the assailants and no action was taken after the match by any of the authorities. Le Saux isn't even gay, he is not guilty of the charge, yet because there was no one else to victimise after Fashanu's death, the year before, bully boys picked on him. To be fair to him, he never said it was wrong to be gay and if he had, he wouldn't have continued to receive homophobic slurs across his 14-year career.

At this match, it was intensified as he played as fullback and would take the throw-ins for Chelsea, so he was right near to the touch line and within spitting distance of us, sitting at the halfway line. We could hear the taunts as well as the comments: 'You take it up the arse', 'Who's the fucking poof in blue?' A line had been crossed that day at the Lane. Yet here was I, Mr Gay Politics, unable to confront the homophobes in my own backyard, in front of my very own eyes and ears. I didn't sleep that night. Even now I recoil from the fact that Fraser was physically sick at the final whistle that evening, as he was so overcome with emotion.

Worse was to come. At a league match the following season against Coventry City, about a dozen of us, not all LGBT, had travelled up to see me; I was then living in Northampton and working as, wait for it, Head of Equalities for the County Council. We were sitting very close to the pitch near the halfway line and were surrounded by about a dozen Spurs fans with, shall we say, views to the right of Genghis Khan, and they weren't afraid to let us and everyone around them know what they thought. Our own black players were routinely called names, Alan Sugar, who was then the unpopular owner of the club, was lambasted as a Jew, and even the women stewards were routinely abused. Many of us wanted to leave at half-time, and some had brought their non-supporting partners to a match for the first time. David's partner Duncan was particularly angry. He was incredulous as to why we should put up with that behaviour and pay extortionate ticket prices to witness such shocking scenes. It was particularly depressing for me after all the times I had watched Coventry City matches whilst I was studying at Warwick University.

League Cup final day in 2008 at Wembley Stadium will always stay in my mind, because it was the first time I plucked up the courage to confront someone for a homophobic remark during a match. We were leading the game 2-1, and deep into added-on time after extra time Chelsea's Didier Drogba was doing everything but bribe the referee to get a free kick or penalty. Talking to the fan in front, we became kindred spirits over Drogba's tactics and woeful cheating. Then out of the blue, he turned around to me and shouted, "And he's an effing faggot". Now just moments away from a much-needed and welcome League Cup final victory, our first in the new Wembley Stadium, David, Vince and Fraser looked at me and yes, like Jonathan Woodgate's header that won us the match, I rose to the occasion. "And so am I," I said. He looked at me incredulously, so I said "I'm a faggot". He turned his back and never spoke to me again. Hopefully the point was made and maybe he'll think again before saying something like that to someone in future.

It had only taken me nearly 40 years of supporting Spurs and 17 years of being a season-ticket holder to challenge homophobia. I hoped and prayed that I'd be able to do it again.

Our league form improved in September with three successive wins against Sunderland 1-0, Crystal Palace with the same score and Manchester City 4-1. We also started our Europa League campaign with a home win against FC Quarabag 3-1 but lost in the League Cup to Arsenal 2-1.

CHAPTER 14

BEING IN EUROPE AND SUPPORTING ENGLAND

✳

OCTOBER 2015

'Spurs are nothing if they're not in Europe.' Those words resonated with me as I travelled to Belgium to see Tottenham Hotspur in yet another attempt to win the Europa League. Despite being favourites and playing in the tournament for the last few seasons, we had got no further than the last 16. Those words were uttered by Bill Nicholson, Spurs' finest manager and one of my boyhood heroes. He managed the first British team to win a European trophy – the Cup Winners' Cup – in glorious style 5-1 against Athletico Madrid in 1963. By coincidence, it was exactly 11 years after his death when Spurs played Anderlecht in the group stage of the competition this year.

The lengthy first round group stage only reduced the field to 32 teams in the knock-out stage. Added to that was the fact that losers from the Champions League get a second and undeserved chance to win in Europe as they enter the second round. It would do well to change the format to a direct knock-out competition – that would certainly have added an edge to this match. Not that that was needed here.

Brussels, situated in Flanders, the Flemish-speaking half of Belgium, is an anomaly, as the language of the city is French. The city is the home of the institutions of the European Union and has the greatest range of bleak, bureaucratic buildings that one can imagine, owing much to the Orwellian style of brutal, modernist architecture. It has more bureaucrats working for government institutions than any other city in the world, including Washington DC. It is not one of my favourite places and despite the quaintness of the Grand Place, the old town square, it has few attractive features. The much-vaunted Mannekin Pis is a big disappointment in more ways than one, especially for a gay man where size is important. Due to my work, however, it's probably my most visited of European cities. I spent most of this week however visiting places outside of the capital like Antwerp and Ghent and was pleasantly surprised by the landmarks that these cities had to offer, despite rail strikes and constant rain.

Belgium is the country where many British servicemen,

including 14 Spurs players, lost their lives during the tumultuous Great War of 1914-18. Ypres hosts the Mannien Gate, which is a centre for British remembrance services during Armistice Day. Waterloo is a short train ride from Brussels and hosts commemorations with the European war of 1815. On this trip, I couldn't help remembering Walter Tull, the first black player to play for Spurs, who lost his life as a soldier in the Great War. Like Bill Nicholson, who wasn't given the knighthood he so justly deserved, he is a hero in my eyes.

In terms of football however, this was only my second visit. The first was in Euro 2000 as an England supporter. I had imagined that I would be seeing England in the quarter-finals, but due to the ineptitude of Kevin Keegan's side, I had to settle for seeing England's conquerors, Romania, play Italy in the last eight. Not that football was my main consideration on that visit though, as I had to spend most of the week apologising to Brussels residents and shopkeepers for the poor behaviour of English fans, who had managed to wreck another international appearance by their sad, pathetic behaviour.

Given that I have had to endure hearing English fans singing 'I'd rather be a Paki than a Turk' the first time I saw an England international, which was against Colombia at Wembley in 1995, many of you might wonder why I'm such a fan of the Three Lions. Well put simply, I'm not going to allow a small-minded bunch of hard-core fascists to dictate to me who and what my identity is. For me, being brought up in England since the age of four, this is the country which I call my home and it's also home for thousands of British-born Asians. Our family were naturalised British citizens, my father worked for the British civil service when we were in Kenya, the place of my birth, and he was promised, as a British passport holder, his place in the UK family. So supporting England as the country where I live comes as naturally to me as supporting Spurs, the club closest to my home in Finchley.

The last time I had visited Brussels it was with great pride, as I presented the celebrations for St George's Day in Bermondsey to the European Union. I wondered on this journey if I ever would return in the future in any work capacity to the city again. Britain was due to vote next year in a referendum on EU membership. We had joined the older version of the EU, the European Economic Community, in 1973, and this decision was confirmed by a referendum two years later. Now many wanted to leave because freedom of movement across the continent had brought migrants into the country. It always bugged me that the media dwelt on this and not the reverse side of the coin, that British people could live and work in other EU countries. This issue of bringing together settled and migrant communities – cohesion as it's called – is a key consideration for the EU, particularly at this time of the displacement of refugees from the Middle East wars and my work reflected that.

Since the 1970s, Bermondsey had seen a march by the National Front on April 23rd. By the time I began working in the area, the march had dwindled to a mere handful of people, many of whom came from the Midlands to walk down Southwark Park Road, the high street in Bermondsey. Working with Millwall's Community Scheme and the local residents, we tackled this problem by hosting the first St

George's Day event as a multi-cultural celebration recognising the patron saint's links (if he did exist) with numerous countries as well as England. That event is still running ten years later – the National Front march no longer happens. The event is celebrated by all communities. So don't tell me there's no black in the Union Jack.

I don't think we will pull the plug on our EU membership simply because we now trade in the largest united market in the world, and if we were to come out, the resulting tariffs we would have to pay would decimate our economy. Also those migrants who come to Britain pay their way and the tax collected from them helps us to secure the welfare system, not least of which is the NHS, which would collapse if all the migrants working for it as GPs, consultants, nurses and other staff had to leave.

For Spurs, our record in Europe, as with England, is also blemished by hooliganism. The most prominent outbreak was in the 1974 UEFA Cup final when playing Feyernoord over two legs. The second leg in Rotterdam was marred by terrible fan violence, which nearly led to the game being abandoned. Poor old Bill Nicholson, who had managed Spurs to UEFA glory against Wolves just two years earlier, had to painfully spend the whole of the half-time period on the PA system pleading with supporters to end the violence. It was a sad and unworthy end to his reign as manger. I remember listening to the match on the radio tuned into Football Special on the BBC Radio 2 channel and crying my eyes out, as this was the first time in Spurs' entire playing history that the club had lost a cup final. It was simply not meant to happen – Spurs and Cup Final appearances were synonymous with winning silverware. I spent ten years trying to erase that memory.

In 1984 Spurs would have probably the most heartening performance of the club's long stay at White Hart Lane in the second-leg of the UEFA Cup final against Anderlecht. The final occurred during my time at Warwick University. I shall never forget that match – the intensity of the atmosphere, the battling spirit of a team harried by injuries as both Glenn Hoddle and Ossie Ardiles had to sit out the final, and the thrilling climax of a penalty shoot-out. Twelve of us from university had formed the North London Society so that we could get the Students' Union to pay for a minibus and driver to take us from Coventry to the match. Even a couple of Gooners from the group had joined us for the occasion, although I don't recall how they managed to acquire tickets. We got our tickets by queuing on the day of the match. It had cost us just 25p each to join the North London Society. There's nothing quite like seeing your own club win a trophy in their own backyard on the drama of a penalty shoot-out. It would be manager's Steve Burkinshaw's final match and the end of an era for both the club and supporters. It remains to this day the finest home match I have attended.

So the match against Anderlecht 31 years later in the successor tournament to the UEFA Cup was a must-see tie. The two games against Anderlecht, the first of which we lost 2-1 and the second at the Lane a fortnight later, which we won by the same score, didn't fail to entertain. It felt like a two-legged tie with both teams playing expansive, attacking football. There was hardly any time to catch breath in both games, which were played at the highest tempo I've known. It was a fitting tribute to the event held in 1984.

I also got the shock of my life when opening the match day programme for the home tie to see that Spurs had featured the story of my trip in 1984, as one of the recollections of that Spurs Glory, Glory Night.

We faltered in October with a 1-1 draw against AC Monaco in the Europa League before losing away to Anderlecht. In the Premiership we drew 2-2 with Swansea away, a match I went to and Liverpool at home 0-0, before picking up a 5-1 win away at AFC Bournemouth.

CHAPTER 15

TO DARE IS TO DO

✷

NOVEMBER 2015

My decision to take up the offer of voluntary severance at the end of June meant that I had to wait before claiming unemployment benefit. It was the first time I had been on the dole since leaving university nearly 30 years before. Then I had spent three months looking for a job, and still after all this time has elapsed, I know the exact number of applications I made and the interviews I was short-listed for (86 jobs and eight interviews) before gaining employment. Ever since then I'd been in work, so I expected that claiming benefit would be an entitlement. It was not quite as easy as that. The system is devoid of any humanity – bleak offices, overworked staff and a stifling bureaucracy. I had first signed on the week before I went to the Anderlecht game, not knowing that if you go abroad you lose your claim, which is fair enough, but you then have to complete the same forms as a new claimant when you return. That shouldn't be too difficult, I thought, but when they lose your forms on the system, you're kept waiting an hour for a timed appointment and then have to complete the forms for a third time, you do begin to lose patience.

I did dip my toe in the job market and had a better ratio for job applications to short lists than I had 30 years ago (12 jobs and four interviews). I was interviewed for similar jobs to those I had undertaken before, and the feedback from my last interview summed up why I wasn't successful in receiving a job offer: 'We didn't think you really wanted the job.' A devastating but essentially true summation. My heart wasn't in any of the jobs I had applied for. I had done my time in local government and needed new opportunities.

To keep my mind off the eventual necessity of having to find a job, I did think of blowing some of my severance money on travelling with the Spurs squad to FC Quarabag, our next opponents in the Europa League. Tottenham were offering fans the opportunity to join the players' flight to Azerbaijan, stay overnight and then to be flown back. I thought it might make good copy for this book, but the cost, I am afraid to say, deterred me from embarking on this endeavour to the outer limits of Europe. Anyone expecting a chapter on Baku, the Azerbajani capital, will therefore be left disappointed, and any snippets of gossip I could have gained from being so close to the first team squad will have to wait for this book's sequel – when the publisher is able to cover the costs of such an extravagance.

November is usually a month for fireworks, so let's throw some fuel on the bonfire. As the club's Latin motto goes, *'audere est facere,'* which means 'to dare is to do'. So let's dare! Many people will I expect be reading this book with a certain amount of fascination about the sexuality of footballers. After all, rumours have been circulating to the effect that the first Premiership player is about to come out or be exposed in a Sunday scandal befitting of the now disgraced rag the *News of the World*. Indeed speculation was so rife this season that two premiership stars would be coming out, one of which, we were led to believe, was a current England international playing for a top five club. Luke Shaw, Manchester United's fullback, seemed compelled to go on social media to discount any such rumours that they meant him: 'I'm not gay,' he said, and we all sighed with relief. Let me state that in my seasons as an out Spurs fan I have heard numerous rumours associated with top flight footballers, even some being quite close to home, which I will address later. I have, however, never met an out Premiership footballer, although I have met one from a lower league.

Before I divulge any secrets, I want to consider the assumption that gay men are not really into the football side of things and are more interested in lusting over the players. To be totally frank, being in a virtually all-male environment and getting close to fellow supporters does have his advantages, especially when we score. In all honesty, however, even in the most dreadful of nil-all draws, my attention is more on how the team is playing than what the players look like. David and I have a code during matches. If one player on the opposing side is cute, I will just say his shirt number and David will take a look. As for our players, there have been one or two that we follow with more attention than others. Let me say here and now that David Ginola wasn't one of them, although I know many lesbians who would die to have his babies! Players who have attracted my attention over the years include David Bentley and Jamie O'Hara.

For what began as a laugh, GFSN in its early years, had an end of season poll of members – the so-called 'Lust List'. In 2001 and in the following year I contacted fellow Spurs fan and Warwick alumni Vivek Chaudary, who was one of the dozen that I had seen help us win on that famous night in 1984. Now *The Guardian's* football correspondent and with his own weekly column *'Digger'*, he publicised the results of the poll. That year, David Beckham won, closely followed by Alan Smith in second place (not the Gooner with the same name), the then Leeds United striker, with another England player, James Beattie, getting the bronze medal. Beckham had always been a favourite, not only because of his looks but because he was one of the first footballers to accept gay sexuality. The next year Liverpool's Michael Owen was top, with team mate Steven Gerrard runner-up. Beckham was again third with my favourite, Joe Cole, fourth.

The closest I have come to having 'sexual relations', as President Clinton once put it in relation to a White House intern, with a footballer from the Premiership, is simply that, though I have had relations with footballer's relatives.

It all began with a threesome with Clayton Blackmore's cousin, or I should say with a person who said he was Clayton Blackmore's cousin. He was certainly as good looking as the Manchester United player, but I was the odd one out in the threesome and the door was eventually closed in my face, so I had to wait for my friends to finish him off, so to speak.

Then there is John Pratt's cousin, which is closer to home. John Pratt scored the first goal I witnessed live at White Hart Lane when we lost 3-1 to Nottingham Forest. He was also the first Spurs player I saw in the flesh whilst he was in a coach travelling to an away match against Newcastle United in the season we were relegated to Division Two. So when my fuck buddy said he was John Pratt's cousin, I was flabbergasted and nearly fell out of the bed. He couldn't of course see why anyone should be that bothered, or in my case, honoured about it. I hope John doesn't mind this connection being revealed. When I met him last season and said I knew his cousin, I could visibly see the double-take.

Gay sex involves a large degree of effort. First, you can't just chat anyone up. I recall my brother saying you could tell a poof by his white polo neck jumper. On this basis Terry lost all respect for the television commentator Barry Davies! Second, at least when I was on the prowl, the venues and places to meet others for sex were often not very safe. Little wonder that when the ITV programme did a piece on gay sex in the 1980s it had to black out the faces of the men they interviewed. My first-ever sexual experience was after I replied to an advert in *Gay Times*; I had a response from a 28-year-old and we met at his home. The only problem was that he was twice my age and I had to run out of the home when his boyfriend came home unexpectedly. So naive I was then that at the time his boyfriend appeared, I said I didn't mind him joining in! It wouldn't have worked, even if I had managed to become a home wrecker, as he admitted to being a Chelsea fan.

So if I did want to practise my sexuality, I had to break the law. One such experience happened when I was oblivious to any attention and another when I had least expected it. It happened on a train on the way to Birmingham for a conference. On the train, I noticed that I was sharing a carriage with one of my childhood heroes, Jack Taylor, the English referee of the 1974 World Cup Final. At the age of 10, I knew that I neither had the talent nor the disposition to be a footballer, but the man in black with the whistle was perhaps a viable option for a career, for a boy who liked being in control and the centre of attention. The memory of the way Taylor handled that match, staying cool to give two penalty decisions, always stayed with me.

Just as I was going to get up from my seat to cross to the opposite table where Taylor was seated, the lad in front me brushed my leg with his. I looked up at him and noticed a smile across his face. I left my leg where it was. This young man was obviously more adept then I had imagined. Before the train arrived at the next station, he had managed to unbutton my flies and make his intentions quite clear. He wanted to finish me off at the next stop, which was Coventry. Pleased with himself, he got up with a wry smirk adorning his face and a nod, asking me to follow. Carefully concealing my sexual endowment with the newspaper I was reading (I was thankful that it was a broadsheet and not a tabloid), I got up and hurriedly said, "Mr Taylor, I just wanted to shake your hand and thank you for giving me so much pleasure." He was slightly taken aback but smiled and said "My pleasure." The lad who had beckoned me couldn't understand what I was up to, but he soon hit the spot in a cubicle on the platform. I got the next train and was, as ever, late for the start of the conference I was travelling to.

'Cottaging', the practice of men having sex with men in public conveniences, wasn't in the understanding of the public domain for much of the post-war period. It was only when the occasional celebrity was found with his trousers down, or a revered actor was confronted by a plain clothes police officer, that the subtle and sometimes not so subtle practice was uncovered. A certain MP, for example, had a 'moment of madness' on Clapham Common. It was the main way of meeting men for casual, no-strings encounters before the day of phone applications such as Grindr.

It was on one such trip to a cottage in the late 1980s that I met an ex-footballer whose career spanned the lower divisions. We did away with any formal introductions and dived into a cubicle. I have to say that it was highly pleasurable. We had the door locked and I had no intention of sharing him with anyone else. He was surprisingly wanton. On seeing me in a football shirt he told me exactly who he had played for and what his name was. A quick perusal of my football annuals when I returned home confirmed his identity. He was playing for a non-league club now, due to an injury cutting short his professional career, but he had started with a top five football squad, although he had failed to make the first team and remained on the bench.

Hardly, for me and hopefully for him, a moment of madness – one of pure, sheer joy instead.

November started off well with a convincing 3-1 win at the Lane against a hapless Aston Villa side and then that 2-1 win against Anderlecht. This was followed by a 1-1 draw against the Gooners at their library. We then smashed the Hammers 4-1 at home and a 1-0 win at FC Quarabag. The last game of the month was a goalless draw at home to Chelsea.

CHAPTER 16

THE THREE WISE MEN

✳

DECEMBER 2015

I was privileged to be invited to the first Spurs' Fans Forum of the season at Lilywhites House, the first phase of the Northumberland Park Development Project – the rebuilding of the stadium into the largest capacity footballing arena in London, with 61,000 spectators able to watch the Spurs. Planning permission was granted, now that an obstinate organisation that was refusing to close as a business had lost its appeal to a compulsory purchase order in the High Court.

If you have kept up until now, you will recall that I had been fortunate enough to have tutored here during last season's LGBT History Month, taking a class on tackling homophobia in football. It was then that I was impressed by the facilities the students had on offer – a world away from the Portakabins that were provided for my sixth form education in the 1980s. During the summer I was also welcomed to a tour of the facilities by the club's Community Foundation as a thank you for undertaking that session. On reflection the students were honest and forthright about how they felt and much more worldly wise than I had been at their age.

Yet when I entered that Fans' Forum I wasn't thinking of my later school years but those much earlier, when in school nativity plans, because of my ethnic appearance, I always played one of the Three Kings. It crossed my mind that Spurs were now entrusted to Three Wise Men – Chairman Daniel Levy, Head Coach Mauricio Pochettino and club captain Hugo Lloris. These were the ones literally bringing frankincense, gold and myrrh to the supporters. For it had been one of our best starts to a Premiership season, with only one loss since the start of the season and that coming in our first game; an unlucky 1-0 at Old Trafford.

Our best match last month had been an emphatic 4-1 win against West Ham, who always seem to treat their away match against us as their most important of the season. You can see why the animosity has built up. In recent years we have poached some of their best players, outbid them for players on their shopping list and then sold them players well after their Premiership sell-buy date. It's no wonder that they are easily wound up at us singing with much glee that 'they've lost their Cup Final – again.'

Envy had broken onto the boardroom as well. An ill-judged last-minute attempt by Levy to scupper the Hammers' plans to move into the Olympic Stadium in Stratford rebounded by making our fans unhappy that we had even contemplated moving outside our own neighbourhood. You could see why the prize of a purpose-built arena in the Queen Elizabeth Park, host to the 2012 Olympics, was tempting for Levy – it would mean public finances would be spent on subsidising the creation of a new football stadium. West Ham, who were always favourites, won the day, but for me and many other supporters, the amount of public subsidy the Hammers will enjoy at the expense of the taxpayer still rankles.

As the combination of Levy, Poch and Hugo marched onto the stage for the assembled fans for a question and answer session, I was struck at the genuine warmth from the audience. Maybe after years of trying, since Venables departed in the fiasco which led to litigation with our previous Chairman, Alan Sugar, I was at last witnessing a dynasty that could bring back the glory days to the Lane. For Daniel had now locked the club's owners into building a first-class stadium which would be second only to Wembley; Poch, at only 43, could well end up staying for many seasons, unlike his predecessors, who always, with the exception of Martin Jol, felt like temporary fixers. In Hugo we had arguably the best goalkeeper in the world and certainly our best since the marvellous Pat Jennings, worth at least a dozen league points a season.

Vince was fortunate to have actually met the great

Irishman Pat, and not in the first place that comes to mind. Like myself, Vince came from a Catholic background and had to pay his respects at the church, which is still opposite the stadium in White Hart Lane. As he was receiving communion, he noticed that the man kneeling next to him had enormous hands – yes, it was Northern Ireland's finest international at mass, on the day of a game. When in Belfast, many football supporters related to this story and the incredible size both of his hands and his heart, a genuine, warm man with hands the size of frying pans.

I couldn't help feeling that some of the plaudits should go to those unseen behind the stage or at least those sitting in the audience. Sitting next to me was Jesu Da Silva, Poch's first team coach, and I noticed that Pochettino would always rely on him for answers before replying to questions, and not always because he sought reassurance that his English was acceptable. And sitting next to him was Donna Marie-Cullen, who I'd met last season, as you may recall, at the Pride in Football Conference. I was impressed fairly early on how well she grasped our issues. She had a shrewd awareness of her brief, was able to make quick decisions and was a master in front of the media. I still think it's a shame that Donna, in a football world of male domination, isn't used to explain the club's position publicly on matters much more frequently, particularly as Daniel seems to be shy of a public persona. With things on the field going so well, the only real anxiety shown by the audience (it wouldn't be a group of Spurs supporters unless they had something to moan about) was over the temporary move of the club's home fixtures in the season after next, whilst the new stadium building took a pace forward.

Chris Paouros from the Proud Lilywhites managed to get in the first question about how the club would react to a player coming out as gay. Hugo shrugged in a charming Gallic way,as if to say what's the problem? Poch sought a translation from his assistant.It was left to Levy to answer the question directly by saying that the club supported diversity and this would never be an issue with Spurs. By then Pochettino had caught up and kept saying "no problem". It was gratifying to see such positivity from1} all three of them1}.

Our bid to scupper the Hammers plans had led to their Board ruling out ground-sharing with us for the 2017-18 season, so only two viable options were left. The first was to move to Milton Keynes, an area where many of our natural supporters live and to use the MK Arena, home of League One side MK Dons (maybe that's why they had sold us Dele Alli?) or to rent out Wembley Stadium. The latter seemed less likely now, as Chelsea had just announced their own plans to rebuild Stamford Bridge and their desire to move into Wembley. Wherever we play however, when we return to Tottenham it won't be to White Hart Lane. It will cost the club going on £750 million to build the new stadium and as part of the financing, naming rights will have to be part of the package. All newly-built stadiums had that attachment – Emirates replaced Highbury and the Amex Stadium was the new home for Brighton and Hove Albion. Yet for all fans it will always be White Hart Lane, whatever the name of the sponsors.

I couldn't help thinking that the stadium deserved to be named after Bill Nicholson, the club's most successful manager by a quantum leap. He was quintessentially the one-club man, despite a brief spell at West Ham after his 16-year tenure as manager came to an end in 1974. In his long career at the club stretching back to the post-war era, he'd also played, coached and scouted for Tottenham, ending up as Club President. The Nicholson Stadium certainly has some ring to it.

Then there are other one-club wonders that I've watched during my time as a supporter at the Lane. Steve Perryman still holds the record for club appearances and from 1969-82 he was a versatile defender-cum-midfield player. He was followed by Gary Mabbutt, who also captained the club and played from 1984-97. Although originally bought from Bristol Rovers, he was to become a legend in his own time, battling through career-threatening injuries, including one especially nasty knock from Justin Fashanu's brother John which nearly left him blinded, and his own long-time medical condition of being diabetic. More recently there has been Ledley King, who played mostly in central defence with again a long-term injury, this one to his knee, making playing a painful pursuit. From 1999 until his retirement in 2012 he was a stalwart for the club. All three wise men should have played for their country (England) more, as between them they only amassed a few caps. They had all played the price for being ahead of their time in my view. They were all great players in a number of positions and all three wore the Captain's armband with pride.

Wouldn't it be great if three wise men each had one side of the stadium named after them –
Perryman, Mabbutt and King. And what, I hear you ask, of the fourth? Well, Walter Tull springs to mind. Unfortunately it will only be in a parallel universe that

those wise men will receive the accolades they so rightly deserve.

On the pitch, things continued in earnest. After a 1-1 draw away at the Hawthorns, we lost 2-1 to Newcastle United at the Lane. We then beat Southampton away 2-0, Norwich City at home 3-0 and finally Watford away 2-1. We also crushed AC Monaco at home 4-1 and qualified with Anderlecht for the knock-out phase of the Europa League.

1970: My brother and I outside our home in Finchley, North London.

1996: David, me, Vince and Fraser in Blackpool.

2008: Six of the 12 of us, including Fraser, David and Vince,
who went to the League Cup Final win.

2014: Meet Spurs legends Paul Allen and John Pratt.

2014: Terry and I catch up before Chelsea park their
bus at White Hart Lane.

2016: With Robert from CSKA Fans against Racism.

2016: With the young EURO 2016 volunteers in Paris.

2017: The Proud Lilywhites meet Gareth Thomas.

CHAPTER 17

UP FOR THE CUP!

✹

JANUARY 2016

As a youngster I looked forward to the start of the new year with gleeful anticipation of the FA Cup. Spurs fans believe it's our cup – we've won it eight times, only once have we lost a final and every year it gives us an opportunity to sing 'Spurs are on our way to Wembley.' Which other club has sold a record on the basis of reaching a Cup Final and then sung it every season since? Chas and Dave must have their names embellished on the trophy, the number of times their career has been resurrected by a Cup Final appearance by the boys from White Hart Lane. Yet we haven't reached an FA Cup final in all the years since I've invested in a season ticket. However, the tingle has always remained there if you're a Spurs supporter when the third-round draw takes place. Expectation is high and White Hart Lane is packed to the rafters if we play at home, putting to shame other clubs' fans who seem to think winning the cup should take second place to a higher position in the Premier League.

This season we drew Leicester City, the side who beat us in the fourth round last year at the Lane. City were then in a real relegation battle, having spent most of the season trapped at the bottom of the league. However, miraculously, they had engineered the Great Escape with a string of victories. Their good form continued into this season and despite a change of manager (actually maybe *because* of a change of manager) the Foxes, 5,000-1 outsiders at the start of the season, were now Premiership leaders. Chelsea had disappeared down the league with a crass loss of form – and their most successful manager in the club's history, Jose Mourinho, had been sacked; Manchester United still seemed to play as if they missed the guile of Sir Alex Ferguson and their city counterparts were unsettled by talk of a new manager. We had also been in form and in taking on these sides we were different compared to last season. We had beaten Manchester City 4-1 at home in September and in November, Chelsea had parked their bus at the Lane in a gutless performance and after scraping a point in a goalless draw, celebrated as if they'd won the match.

Leicester and Spurs have a fine tradition of matches against each other and a rivalry which was cemented in the 1960s. We beat City to win the double in 1961, 2-0 at

Wembley. Yet in that same season Leicester was the first team to beat us at home in the League. Leicester always seemed to be the bridesmaid in that decade. They ended that season sixth behind Burnley in fourth, who we beat the following year in 1962 to retain the trophy, and City also lost the 1963 FA Cup final to Manchester United. They did eventually win the League Cup in 1964 before losing it again the following season. They capped off an unlucky decade with another FA Cup final disappointment against Manchester City in 1969.

As fate would have it we were drawn to play Leicester near our home League fixture against the Foxes. With us in fourth place, that was a real six-pointer in our pursuit of a Champions League place. First though the Cup match, and what a thrilling game. It went end to end, and must have been great watching it as a neutral, but not so good for the nerves if you were actually there and supporting one side. We dominated the first 20 minutes and could – and should – have taken advantage. Yet City slowly powered their way back into the game to lead 2-1 after being a goal down. They were the finished article as far as away performances go – solid in defence and breaking with a pace and determination that showed real team spirit.

All season, commentators had been raving about Jamie Vardy scoring in six consecutive games and setting a new Premiership record and Riyad Mahrez, whose sublime skill had not gone unnoticed. Yet I was genuinely surprised at the depth of quality in their side from Mark Drinkwater in midfield to Robert Huth in defence – they certainly weren't short of fitness. I have to say that they deserve their position at the top if their performance against us was anything to go by: easily the best and most difficult side we had encountered at the Lane so far this season. To win the Cup though, you do need a bit of luck and we gained that in stoppage time with a fortunate penalty duly scored by Kane which sealed a 2-2 draw.

The next game was back at the Lane and could we outfox Leicester again, this time for League points? Both sides played on paper stronger sides than the first encounter, and this time our luck ran out. Leicester won 1-0 and edged us. They were still on top with away games against Man City and the Gooners yet to come. For us it looked like we would have to settle for revenge at the King Power Stadium in the third-round replay. Our record playing the same team in the League after or before a cup game isn't that good. I recalled losing 1-0 to Southampton at their place in the League before witnessing us capitulate 4-0 to the Saints in the FA Cup a couple of days later. I remember being told by a local that there was nowhere worth eating Sunday lunch in the town and that we should get out into the New Forest. To be honest, I wished we had never come, as our team failed to show up that day, in what still remains my worst away match performance. That was in 2003 and it was karma for the Saints, as we had poached their manager, Spurs legend Glenn Hoddle, to coach us, a couple of years before. He really had lost the support of the players at that game and his tactical awareness was about as good as his political correctness – dire. It reminded me of the 4-0 mauling a Hoddle-managed Chelsea side had received in the 1994 FA Cup Final – he just froze, unclear and unaware what to do to stem the onslaught from Manchester United. Since then of course we had again gone back to the Saints to poach our present Head Coach – thank heavens we hadn't drawn Southampton this season!

That cup trip to the St Mary's stadium was probably the last we had done as a group. There was a time stretching back to Blackpool in the third round in 1991 when we would make a weekend of it. That first trip to Bloomfield Road was infamous for the game nearly being postponed due to high winds; a walk on the promenade nearly led to me being lost at sea!

In 1994 we all travelled up to Ipswich for an FA Cup match and nearly missed the kick-off enjoying a pub lunch – we had to rush out and I left my wallet there. The game wasn't memorable – we lost 3-0. During the second half, many of my friends thought they heard my name on the Tannoy system. I ignored it, thinking that they only used the system to notify emergencies such as 'your wife is having a baby', and as that was unlikely to happen to me, I thought they must have mentioned someone else. It turned out that it was for me, as some kind Ipswich fan had collected my wallet and returned it to the club. In the end the club posted the wallet to me.

The following year we went all the way – well almost – and so did I! In the quarter-finals we met Liverpool and the match, memorable for Klinsmann's last-minute winner, and he wasn't the only one who scored. I managed it on the way to the match with a Liverpool fan at Toddington services on the M1. And they say I watch Spurs for the love of the game. As I kept everyone waiting, my friends noticed that the lad I had just 'met' had a smile as wide as the Mersey Tunnel and I couldn't stop smiling all day either. It was smashing of the Liverpool supporters to give us praise after we'd won.

They're a different type of football fan at Anfield – simply the best.

In 1996 there was another first for me, an abandoned match. We were drawn against Nottingham Forest, who had already got their revenge for our 1991 FA Cup final win by beating us in the League Cup semi-finals in 1992, after the home tie had been delayed due to a bomb scare. Now in the FA Cup, the game at the City Ground was abandoned after only 13 minutes due to heavy snow. It took us hours to get home that night, though the journey was made a little more comfortable as we were able to follow the team bus home.

The games against Leicester now are nothing like the ones we had against Wimbledon in 1999. We played the Dons five times in the space of a month, once in the league, twice in the FA Cup and over two legs in the semi-final of the League Cup. We were successful in winning both cup matches against them and as we've already noted we went on to beat Leicester in the League Cup Final but lost to Newcastle United in the FA Cup semi-final. For Wimbledon it signalled the beginning of the end of the club. They had needed either one or both cup final appearances to plug holes in their finances. Outings in the next decade amounted to little more than continuing disappointment in FA Cup semi-finals. Another three occasions followed, losing to Woolwich in Sol Campbell's last game for us in 2001, Portsmouth at Wembley in 2010 and Chelsea two years later.

Yet I fancied this trip to the replay in Leicester. I had thoroughly enjoyed the first match and I also had a willing mum who would accompany me for the weekend, but not to the match of course. She had stood in for my friends for away matches a couple of seasons now. Our first was at Stoke City when, thinking I had loads of time, I got to the ground with only fifteen minutes to spare until kick-off, thinking it would be easy to park my car. Of course it wasn't, and I missed Bale's extraordinary goal, getting into the ground just fifteen minutes before half-time.

Mum and I had now become best friends, and I could confide in her all my feelings. She had come a long way for a devout Catholic who had thought of becoming a nun, but it wasn't always like that. The issue of my sexuality first arose when I was 14, as you will read later, and again when I was about to graduate and she found my boyfriend's picture in my wallet. I then came out and the following Christmas refused to come home, spending it with him, rather than with my parents. After tearful phone calls and letters, we came to the conclusion that being gay wasn't a temporary phase, as she had hoped. Like so many things in life, my parents took advice from a priest, who thankfully was 'on message', saying that my sexuality was an issue for me and me alone, and not to judge me.

The previous time I had been to Leicester was also for the FA cup in 2002. I had family connections with the city. Leicester has a high concentration of Goans, and my godfather first landed in the city after departing Kenya. He was such a charming old fella who I really warmed to, becoming a surrogate Granddad. Unlike my dad, he had a keen interest in football and will always live long in the memory as he was the first to give me my first ever football annual– the Rothmans' Yearbook in 1972. One of the city's MPs, Keith Vaz, was also a Goan and we had become friends through the Labour Party. I was also keen to visit the new exhibition space for King Richard III and to see a rejuvenated city. Certainly in the 14 years since I had last visited, the city had undergone a transformation, clearly now adapting itself from the image of a small market town to a worthwhile city break destination.

The atmosphere inside the stadium was electric – you could see why many clubs had come here and gone away with nothing. Yet ultimately, I wasn't to be disappointed. If we had all the luck in the first match, and were a bit unfortunate in the League match, we deserved to win in this third and last encounter. It was a glowing performance; the team played with no fear – looking steady at the back and inspired up front. We won 2-0, a scoreline which belied our dominance. It dawned on me that this was like no Spurs team I'd known previously – we had quality, but now we had added a mental toughness. We were clinical, dare I say it comfortable, after we scored first.

It was then that I thought we could really do something special this season – go one better and reach a FA Cup Final after six consecutive failures at the semi-final stage. If we could beat the League leaders in their own backyard, then on our day, why not?

Outside of that League loss to Leicester, our league form was mixed, so it did look as if glory in one of the cups, seemed to be the more realistic option for silverware. We drew with Everton away 1-1 and beat struggling Sunderland 4-1 at the Lane and then Crystal Palace away 3-1. In the FA Cup we swept aside Colchester United away 4-0 in the fourth round.

CHAPTER 18

MANCHESTER: WHERE THE RAIN SHINES

✳

FEBRUARY 2016

Manchester must figure more than once in any history of a supporter. It is, after London, as many Mancunians would claim, the centre for the nation's preoccupation with football history and heritage. However, what credit it has gained for football it loses for me with the weather, unless of course you like it raining – and I don't mean showers, it pours and pours. I can't recall a weekend in the city when we've travelled up for a match which hasn't been wet, sometimes showery and occasionally like being on the set of a monsoon.

For me Manchester's significance lay in the fact that our home game against City in 1990 was the first match I attended as a member of GFSN. It was the first game of that season and 12 gay men supporting both teams met up after the game to celebrate a Spurs win. A night of drinking and fun followed, with me and several others ending up lost on Hampstead Heath (don't ask why, but it was a week after my birthday). This was followed up by a visit to Maine Road for the away fixture that December. The weekend would be the first of a long line of annual GFSN Social Weekends before they moved to the end of the season. Maine Road was the only ground where you had to pay a protection fee to youngsters so that you wouldn't return to your car unable to drive home because the tyres were slashed. The ground was in the Moss Side area of the city, which was noted for its multi-cultural character. It therefore had the advantage of being in Balti country and after the match it was always a tradition to have a curry.

Two or three curried visits later, in 1992-93, as I have mentioned already, we played City in the FA Cup. After the match, safe in the knowledge that I had paid a quid to a scally to keep care of my car before the game and sure that we would get a police escort after the game, I revelled in the jubilant atmosphere that Spurs were on their way to Wembley for another semi-final despite all the hostility from the home supporters in the stadium. I should have been afraid, very afraid, because as soon as we were let out of the ground, the police vanished. One of them had the audacity to say to me, "Mind how you go" as he went his jolly way.

Perhaps overtime payments stopped 30 minutes after the match, or more likely the Greater Manchester Police couldn't be bothered if a few cockneys got the shite kicked out of them. Well that's what happened to me. With no capacity to run I just tumbled over and let them get on with it. What probably saved me was my pacifist posture; if I'd tried to retaliate – not that I would know how to – I would have probably ended up in hospital.

Since moving into their new stadium, the rebuilt venue for the 2002 Commonwealth Games, which had seemed to rejuvenate the city centre much as the Olympics had done for Barcelona ten years earlier, City's reputation had increased in line with the wealth of its new owners. City had certainly taken campaigning to their heart, being the first Premiership club to designate a specific game against homophobia two seasons ago and last season, as I noted, wearing T-shirts against homophobia, in the same way that Kick it Out campaigners had got most clubs to challenge racism. This year they really cranked up the volume by flying the rainbow flag from the stadium, not just a banner in the ground, and by introducing the Canal Street Blues pre-match and at half time with us, the Proud Lilywhites, they certainly increased the visibility of the issue.

Football on the pitch at the Eithad, as it is now called, continued to give oodles of pleasure. Spurs won, coming back from being a goal down to win 2-1. We had still only lost one league game away all season – that first game against City's red neighbours at Old Trafford, who had since slipped out of contention. It was also the first time we had done the double against the Blues for a while, coming on top of our 4-1 win earlier at the Lane. It meant that we were now second only to Leicester City in the Premiership. The day was made perfect by seeing our players wearing the Football v Homophobia T-shirts for the first time in their pre-match warm up.

Then I made the fatal mistake every Spurs fan makes when things get like this, which isn't that often. We puff out our chests and crow as proud as a cockerel. A few seasons before we had gone 12 points clear of the Gooners in a race for a Champions League place and I had provocatively placed on Facebook a warning for the Woolwich fans to 'Mind the Gap'. From that day on our lead was overcome, and despite ending fourth and in a Champions spot we were pipped to the post when a Drogba penalty bounced Chelsea into the competition above us by winning the trophy. So instead of learning my lesson, what did I do? I went to the bookies and put a fiver on Spurs doing the double. Well, why not? We'd beaten the favourites in the League – twice – and knocked the League leaders out of the Cup. I couldn't have been more wrong – again! After all the year didn't end in a 1, did it?

Within a week of our win against Man City, which would be our most impressive performance of the season, we had been knocked out of the FA Cup by Crystal Palace, losing 1-0 at home. It was a game we deserved to win. On the day however we did everything but score. At one time the ball even hit one post, went all the way across the goal line and hit the other! Palace would go on to meet and lose to Manchester United in the final, a repeat of the 1990 one.

Then I received some good news to soften the blow of losing that fiver. I heard on the grapevine that FSE had been granted money to establish a pan-European project to challenge homophobia in the run-up to, and during, the Euro 2016 tournament. They were therefore seeking an anti-discrimination project adviser for the six months up until after the football championships in France. After taking advice, I applied and was delighted to hear that I had been short-listed for interview.

About to board a plane to head off to Hamburg, where the FSE headquarters were and where I expected to be interviewed, I was stopped in my tracks. "This is the 21st century, Darryl, haven't you heard of Skype?" they said. Er no, I hadn't, but luckily a friend had and talked me through the three easy steps of Skype. Get a computer, download the app and invite people to connect and I was there – in front of a panel some of whom I had met in Belfast and Zürich.

I was convinced they wouldn't appoint me. I was barely able to speak two words of conversational French, let alone count to three in German. So I was left dumbstruck when I was told that I had got get the job and the following week I booked a flight for Hamburg.

In the league things went much better. We beat Norwich City away 3-0, Watford 1-0 at home and Swansea 2-1. In the Europa League, we did better than last season, by drawing 1-1 with Fiorentina in the first leg of the round of 32.

CHAPTER 19

AN ON-SCREEN PERFORMANCE

✳

MARCH 2016

Suddenly I had become an international traveller – well, at least a continental one. I had to travel once a month to Hamburg for an overnight stay for a following day's team meeting. The rest of the time I worked from home. I celebrated my elevation to these dizzy heights by booking a trip to see Spurs at Dortmund. After a convincing 3-0 win in the home tie against Fiorentina, we had been drawn against the Germans in the last 16 of the Europa League.

Before the match and exactly one year after we lost to

Chelsea at Wembley, David and I had been fortunate enough to get tickets for the première of a film, *The Pass*, which was about a closeted professional footballer. It had been a hit as a stage play at the Royal Court Theatre and the film kept the same lead actor in the role of the gay footballer, the delicious Russell Tovey. Now if there is a perfect model for a possible boyfriend for me, look no further than him. Russell had come out in an interview a few years ago and I had seen him on stage. The film version was, I have to say, a bit of a disappointment, as it didn't widen out the play but followed the text and scenes almost word-to-word. It could have done so much more, showing new scenes at matches, in the dressing room and with club officials and managers, but it failed to do so. I came very close to Tovey on the red carpet, but for once, I was too star-struck to say anything.

That wasn't the situation when I met another gorgeous actor, Danny Dyer, after appearing in a 2008 revival of Howard Pinter's play *The Homecoming* at the Almeida Theatre. After the show I went up to him, thanked him for baring all on the front page of gay magazine *Attitude* some time earlier, and said, "We'll be playing your lot at the weekend," referring to our upcoming match against West Ham.

"You're gay Spud fans then," he said, looking at me and David. "That must be difficult. Respect."

"You should come and do a documentary on us for your series, the Football Factory," I replied.

He winked and said "That would be blinding."

Unfortunately I didn't get his number, but a couple of years later I made it to a première of one of his films, *City*

Rats, and saw him whilst I was brazenly sitting in the front circle row with a bevy of his female fans giving it large, as he would say! This time he did give me a wink, slightly bemused. The offer is still there, Danny.

I had no idea where Dortmund was; all I knew was to expect that the atmosphere at the stadium would match, if not exceed, the one I experienced earlier that year at the Allianz Arena in Munich. The stadium had been redeveloped for the 2006 World Cup finals after playing host to matches in the 1974 tournament. At this point it may seem that this journal has developed into a travelogue of German stadia and their cities. It just goes to show that you can never be sure where Spurs will play next. Out of the FA Cup and after losing to Leicester City at home in the Premiership, our only real chance of silverware would be the Europa League. We had gone one round better than last season, as we had done in the FA Cup this season, by getting through to the last 16. Our opponents like us were second in their domestic league. There the similarity ended. As I was to learn, it wasn't just their stadium that was in a different class to ours.

Normally I would prepare a rough itinerary of the trip and try to pack in much as I could to a visit which, as I've already mentioned previously with other trips, normally lasts about four nights – a couple before and a couple after the match on Thursday. Because of rushing around confirming my new job and travelling to Hamburg to sign the contract, I hadn't had much opportunity to do so. As things would work out, the enjoyment of my visit was better for being ill-prepared. For example, as I got off the train in Dortmund on my first day visiting the city, what a sight to behold for a football fan, now working for football supporters in a professional capacity – a gleaming new football history museum. Certainly on a par with ours in Manchester, the German version was only a couple of years old and centred on the nation's four wins in the World Cup (East Germany and the 1945-89 partition is hardly given a mention). You'll gather by now that given my first football memory was the 1970 World Cup in Mexico, where the Brazil team was the first time I had seen so many Black players in the most talented international side in history, I do, FIFA corruption aside, love the final tournaments. I used to rush home from primary school to catch the 1974 finals and was inconsolable when a school trip to Germany got in the way of me watching the 1978 final.

Anyway we get slightly ahead of ourselves, as the first great German victory was the Miracle of Berne – the 1954 final won against the red-hot favourites Hungary in Switzerland. Adidas, the German shoe manufacturer, takes the credit, as on a muddy and wet pitch the use of their new football boots gave the Germans a distinct advantage over the favourites from Hungary. The museum is as meticulous as the German team's preparation for each tournament. They would win on home soil, twenty years later, in Munich in the Olympic stadium I visited earlier this year. In 1974, with England having not even qualified, I supported the West Germany side, as it then was, of Gerd Muller, Franz Beckenbauer and my main man, Paul Breitner. It was well known that Breitner was a bit of a radical bohemian and his leftist politics enthralled me. In fact I spent a lot of my childhood being enraptured by German football and politics. I looked at the SDP governments of Willy Brandt and his successor Helmut Schmidt as templates for the Labour administrations of Harold Wilson and James Callaghan in 1970s Britain to follow.

Something changed – I think it was the smugness of Helmut Kohl when he was on friendly terms with Margaret Thatcher in the 1980s – that ended my love affair with Germany. So the 1990 win against Argentina, their third victory, is marred for me by us being knocked out in the semis on penalties. By the way, the 1966 defeat to England at Wembley only gets a fleeting mention in the museum's artefacts, with claims that the team was robbed by a Russian linesman – how could they think that? Then as you leave the building you're bang up to date with the 2014 victory in Brazil against the Argentinians again. Surprisingly there's little mention of their greatest night, the 7-1 humiliation of the host nation in the semi-final tie of that championship.

The ground itself lived up to expectations. It was just as immense as the Munich stadium, but there the similarity ended. The noise and atmosphere generated by their Kop end, which on Bundesliga dates is all standing, is a wonder to behold and is called the Yellow Wall. The only difference that put me off slightly were the fences around the ground, something that fortunately has seen the light of day in England.

Then the unexpected happened, as in my new role I had been put in touch with the Dortmund fan club which wanted to interview me for their fanzine before the match. Slightly taken aback, I agreed to meet them before entering the ground. I arrived very early, around 5 pm, for an 8 pm kick-off and after meeting fellow supporters of the LGBT supporters group, Rainbow Borussia, who I had met in Zürich, I met up with the supporters' representative. What I didn't know was that he wanted to interview me on the big screen in the stadium on the gantry. Even Spurs' former player, now turned BT Sports pundit, Jermaine Jenas, only got to go pitch side.

I have the highest regard for Jermaine, both as a Spurs player of much flair and as a TV summariser who never fails to support our team. As I saw him pitch side, I recalled the barracking he had received from some of our own supporters. If we lose, there's always some bright spark who would blame one player and if that player makes a mistake, it is highlighted and blown out of all proportion when compared to those made by his fellow team players. Jenas was put into this category and unfortunately his sexuality was also questioned. Watching Spurs away, and even sometimes at home, I witnessed the barrage of slurs Jenas had to face, such as, 'What do you expect when we play a queer?'

Jermaine has addressed some of these homophobic comments recently. He has said that he could hear them and put it down to his friendship with Arsenal players such as Ashley Cole. I also think that some supporters can't deal with players showing that they are cultured, have a brain and aren't all stereotypical 'hard men'.

So for the first time I was on the big screen on a match day and talking about the Proud Lilywhites and other things football-related. As I walked away after the interview, which thankfully was conducted in perfect English, and walked towards the Spurs end I thought 'well that's pretty amazing, I have 'come out' to tens of thousands of people'. Slightly nervous and disconcerted, I walked to my seat, but no one seemed to notice, except an Asian man slightly older than myself who had brought his family to the game, who gave me a much-needed thumbs up and cheery wave. The spirit of my late father I know guides me every day, and I couldn't help feeling this was more than just a symbolic coincidence.

The rest of the 90 minutes was largely forgettable from a Spurs point of view, except for the first ten when we managed to keep up with the blistering pace of the opposition and thirty minutes into the game, when a mass herd of Spurs fans suddenly entered our side and cluttered the gangways, with many of our own stewards clearly distraught. Then it dawned at me that once again Spurs fans travelling away from home had been targeted by some of the worst excesses of foreign policing and stewarding. As I was to learn after the match, many had been sent by police to the wrong entrance far from the away end, and when they finally returned, only to find the turnstiles closing, police had used pepper spray, in an entirely unprovoked and unnecessary attack. It brought back memories of that attack in Seville in 2007 when we played in the quarter-finals of the UEFA Cup against a side which went onto win the trophy. Then, as I've already said, we had been targeted at half time by baton-wielding Spanish police and even our own stewards and a wheelchair user had been left battered. After this game, however, I was determined to do something about it, and now as an employee of Football Supporters Europe we joined up with the Tottenham Hotspur Supporters Trust to complain, and Dortmund was charged by UEFA.

The one criticism I had of our team that night was of Pochettino's selection of players. He rested many first team choices for Sunday's match against the bottom side Aston Villa. We were outplayed and lost 3-0. Many of us who had seen this before, with managers playing weakened sides on a Thursday away match (remember Salonika?) couldn't believe it, and nor could the Dortmund fans, who thought, rightly, that we weren't giving and showing them the respect they deserved. I still think that if the spine of our team, including Dier, Kane and Alli (who was suspended) had played instead of say Ryan Mason, Josh Onomoah and Heung-Min Son, we might have made a match of it. The return leg proved to be a formality, as we lost that 2-1 and went out. Now only the opportunity of a top four finish was at hand. I still thought the title was beyond us and Leicester was some seven points ahead of us.

The month ended with an international break. As an England fan, I took great delight from the fact that five Spurs players had made the squad for two matches, the first against, yes you've guessed it, Germany in Berlin. Four of the five made the team on the night: Eric Dier, Dele Alli, Danny Rose and leading Premiership scorer Harry Kane with the fifth, Kyle Walker, on the bench as one of the substitutes. I hadn't watched an England match for ages, but I decided that this was too good an opportunity, as a Spurs supporter, to miss. And how correct I turned out to be. Spurs had now passed Everton as the club with the most capped England players of all time. What a night to remember, so much so that for me it almost wiped away the memory of that much-maligned 1970 quarter-final tie against West Germany in Mexico. Coincidentally I had been reading Alan Mullery's autobiography at the time and was incredulous that that result was overturned in a highly symmetrical way by the Spurs contingent. Two nil down, England conspired to beat the reigning World Champions 3-2 by two goals scored by Spurs players – Kane of course and Dier, who popped up with a winning header.

For me, in a season when many players have shone at Spurs, Eric Dier is worth more than a mention. This is where Pochettino has got it so right. Give him his due, when the Head Coach decided that Eric could play a holding role in midfield, many of us doubted his wisdom and thought this was, at best, a money-saving option. Now, not only had he played more times than any other outfield player, his first goal for his country had ended up being the winning one. Dier, for me, has all the potential of a Dave Mackay or Steve Perryman, who would replace Alan Mullery in the Spurs side, and more recently Ledley King, who like Dier, could play just as well as a centre-back or as a defensive midfielder. Alan Mullery, who played in a similar position and was one of two players to score in that defeat in Mexico, would I thought be ecstatic as I was. I was sad to hear that the other scorer from the 1970 match in Mexico, Martin Peters, now aged 72, had been recently diagnosed with Parkinson's disease.

As fate would have it, I unexpectedly met Mullery a week before the international. I have a ritual before each game; park the car in the same place, buy a programme from the same vendor and visit the Spurs megastore (even if I don't want to buy something). The latter brought an added bonus before the match against Bournemouth as I noticed that two legends from the team I remember following in the 1970s were there signing autographs – Alan was with Phil Beale, who for me was rather like Toby Alderwierald in the present side: reliable, a team player who gave his all, but was outshone by his partner in defence, Mike England, as Toby is with the ebullient Jan Verthongen. I thanked Phil and said to Alan that his autobiography was one of the most interesting reads in the field of sports writing. And I really meant it. He opens up to his fears and shows a vulnerability that most players today would never dream of owning up to. It also helps if you write your memoirs after a reasonable passage of time, unlike today when players feel the need to publish theirs when they are still in their 20s.

In the Premiership, we lost to the Hammers 1-0 in their last match in the Boleyn before they moved to their new ground next season. We beat Bournemouth at home 3-0 and Aston Villa away 2-0. Yet these wins came after dropping vital points – despite Harry scoring – against the Gunners in an enthralling 2-2 draw. Leicester's lead was cut to five points.

CHAPTER 20

FEELING THE BLUES

✳

APRIL 2016

At the beginning of this book I told you how I had become a Spurs fan and how my brother had opted for the dark side that was at Stamford Bridge. This didn't stop him trying to convert me. Terry took me to a number of games in the mid-70s and one in particular stands out in April 1978, ironically, given what I would experience, just one day before St George's Day. It was Chelsea v Wolverhampton Wanderers and George Berry was playing for the away team. Berry was of Jamaican heritage and played with a distinctive afro hairstyle. I recall being utterly ashamed by the supporters around me who used the N word and called out all manner of racist words against him. Had they not noticed that we – two Asian guys – were sitting right next to them and were likely to be as offended? Of course I had encountered racism at school, in my neighbourhood, on the street, but never with this ferocity and cruelty. I decided that day to perm my hair and a couple of years later I went to a hairdresser's and got it done.

My next venture to the Bridge was in December 1990 and we had grounds for optimism as we were challenging at the top of Division One and had come third the season before. We had also beaten the Blues at their ground last season. How was I to know that that match was the last time we would beat Chelsea until 2002? I often ask myself if I had known then, what I do now, would I have bothered getting a season ticket in 1991? The answer is yes – probably! We lost the match 3-2 and it was the first in a series of 26 during which Chelsea would remain unbeaten by us. The match is also memorable in that I didn't get to the Bridge in time to meet my fellow Spurs fans, but I was lucky – if that's the right word – to get in by bumping into some Chelsea friends I worked with at the time, including Paul Macey, who I mentioned earlier. They sold me a spare ticket they had in the West Stand. So I had paid for the match twice and now had to watch the game with the home supporters. I got increasingly fed up with having to cheer lamely when a Chelsea player tackled or won the ball in an attempt to disguise my true allegiances; the last straw came when they scored their third goal. I got up but didn't cheer. A police officer noticed this and I think it was an offence in those days for an away fan to sit in the wrong end. He touched me on my shoulder and whispered, "Don't worry mate, I'm a Spurs fan and I've got your back."

It wasn't long before I was back – in February 1991 for a League Cup tie which we drew 0-0. Again for some reason that I can't recall, I had to sit in the home stand – a glutton for punishment. I remember the night clearly, despite the uninteresting scoreline, as it was the night British forces invaded Kuwait in the first Gulf War. In total denial that the multi-national force assembled to defeat Saddam Hussein's illegal occupation and annexation of Kuwait included Muslim combatants, the Chelsea hordes kept singing the whole night 'If you all hate Muslims clap your hands.' In fact the highlights of the game were never shown on television, as live coverage of the Gulf War replaced that programme. It was particularly chilling for me, as I had changed planes only three years earlier in Kuwait and the airport was the scene of much hand-to-hand combat.

Fully expecting to win the replay, we lost 3-0 and this time I had matched the favour done my Chelsea work colleagues by buying them two tickets for the Shelf, which was still standing in those days. My gay Spurs friends were also with me and they participated in the smoke that was handed out. I don't know if this was too hard as I didn't take a draw, but one of them left when the third Chelsea goal went in and no lie, I never saw him at the Lane again until I came across him on Facebook 20 years later.

The next visit to Stamford Bridge was while the away end was being reconstructed in light of the Taylor report's need for all-seater stadiums. Again we lost 2-0, but it was memorable in that I bumped into a friend from university,

Tim Vickery. Tim was a stalwart of the Warwick University Labour Club and I heard he had become a comedy sketch show writer after graduating five years ago. He told me that on the Monday after the match he was leaving for good, and not only because the Spurs couldn't stop losing to Chelsea (I sincerely hope his other gags were better than that) but because he had met a Brazilian girlfriend and he was returning with her to South America and was determined to learn Portuguese. The rest as they say is history, as he got his wish to become a freelance football journalist and ended up as the BBC's South America Football Correspondent, hosting some of their coverage of the 2014 World Cup.

I ventured back to the Bridge when the Matthew Harding Stand opened in October 1996. Harding was a director of the club and was a fans' favourite to take over the club before he died in a helicopter crash a short time before the new North Stand was reopened. It was meant to be a game played in a family atmosphere, full of respect for the man. However it turned sour on the day, at least for me, and I vowed never to return. I went to the match with one of my friends from the gay supporters' group who was taunted because she supposedly looked like Whoopi Goldberg. Neither of us have ever returned to the ground. Just for the record we lost again: 3-1. So no more for me the trip up the King's Road. I had to settle for watching Chelsea beating us at the Lane.

When Christian Gross replaced the mid-table mediocrity of Gerry Francis as Head Coach in 1997, a lot was expected from the Swiss technocrat. He was billed as one of the thoughtful European coaches brought into Spurs to modernise our approach to fitness, diet and tactics in the wake of an ever-increasing injury list under Francis. In many respects it was Spurs trying to emulate Arsene Wenger at Woolwich. We all should have known better, because when his assistant failed to gain a work permit, Gross was as good a coach as his name suggests. His first match at the Lane ended in a humiliating 6-1 defeat to Chelsea, the lowest point in my season-ticket history of watching the Lilywhites. There was nothing Proud in that performance.

When Alan Sugar finally sold his controlling interest in the club, 1}to ENIC and Daniel Levy took over the reins of the club, everyone drew a big sigh of relief. Furthermore, the arrival of Glenn Hoddle to replace ex-Gunner and ex Chelsea player George Graham was met with universal approval. Here was the lad from the youth ranks in the 1970s to Spurs' best player in the 1980s, returning as coach after a time managing England and Chelsea in the 1990s. His crowning glory as Spurs boss came in 2002 when he led us to our first appearance at Cardiff's Millennium Stadium, the home of League Cup finals in the era when Wembley was being rebuilt. On the way we trounced Chelsea in the semi-final second leg at home 5-1, winning 6-3 on aggregate. Everyone had expected us to roll over after losing the first leg 2-1. It was the first time we had beaten Chelsea in 12 years, in any competition. We went onto lose to Blackburn Rovers in the final, as the label of favourites never suits Spurs. Worse was to happen later that season as Chelsea got sweet revenge by roundly seeing us off in the FA Cup quarter-final, 4-0. The writing was on the wall for Hoddle and he was sacked not long into the following season.

The curse of the Blues, at least for home games, was finally put to the sword by a swaggering performance in 2006 by Martin Jol's side, which won 2-1, a score line which belittled our overall performance on the day. We went one better with his successor Juande Ramos lifting the League Cup in 2008 by beating Chelsea 2-1 and keeping intact our winning record at Wembley against the Blues. We would also win two more times at home, but that win at the Bridge always eluded us.

To make matters worse, Harry Redknapp's tenure as our manager was sealed when we were humiliated 5-1 in the FA Cup Semi-final at Wembley in 2012, which meant we had equalled Chelsea's record of losing six FA Cup Semi-finals in consecutive appearances at this stage of the competition.

Payback of a kind was given last season when we beat Chelsea – the eventual Champions of the Premier League – 5-3 at home. So1} with that improving record and our second place in the League with Chelsea in mid-table obscurity for once, it seemed that our time had come. In our preceding two League matches, we had beaten a poor Manchester United team 3-0 and pulverised Stoke City at their ground, 4-0. However in the match before our trip to Stamford Bridge we played nervously and stuttered at home to West Bromwich Albion, drawing 1-1 and dropping two valuable points. It was the most important match of our season. We needed to win to keep our chances of overtaking Leicester in first place. All seemed to be fine, we were 2-0 up at half-time, and then our nerve went. Half-time saw more than the usual scuffles in the tunnel and at full-time there was an attempt by Dembele to gouge the eye of an opponent. The atmosphere before the match had not been helped by several Chelsea players saying they didn't want us, as their London rivals, to win the League and that they would rather see it go to the East Midlands. Considering that they had to play City in the last game of the season, this was a scandalous thing to say –they were virtually admitting that they would scupper our chances even if we were to win by lowering their standards against the Foxes.To be fair though, these tactics in undermining us worked – our nerves frayed in the second half and we only drew 2-2. A point wasn't good enough and we bagged another record – the team with the most players booked in a match in the Premiership era-nine. Dembele would also be suspended and join Alli on the sidelines.

The final two games were awful. We lost at home to Southampton 2-1despite clinching Champions League qualification, and then we were bizarrely thrashed 5-1 away at St James's Park. This meant that already relegated Newcastle United had done the double over us. Even worse, we missed out on being runner-up to Woolwich, of all teams – by one point. It is now 21 years since we finished a season higher than the Gooners and 55 since we ended up second in the top flight. We drew some consolation from Harry Kane winning the Golden Boot and Dele Alli the PFA Young Player of the Year – the award Harry won last season. I have still not seen any 'highlights' of the Newcastle game and this time, it isn't due to any war coverage on television.

Riyad Mahrez of Leicester, a Muslim, won the Player of the Year in the same week that a Muslim won the vote for London Mayor – so at least if records for Spurs haven't changed, much else has changed for the better.

Just for the record in the Premiership, we drew 1-1 with Liverpool away, beat Manchester United at home 3-0 and Stoke City 4-0 away. We then stumbled to a 1-1 draw against WBA at the Lane before the 2-2 draw at the Bridge.

PART 3

✳

2016/17

CHAPTER 21

LE WEEKEND IN PARIS

✹

MAY 2016

Disappointment at not ending the season as runners-up soon dissipated, as I had to turn my attention to the EUROS, or the European Football Championships, to give them their full title. As part of FSE I joined with partner organisations in Austria, Slovenia, France and Italy to be active within the Queering Football project. Funded through the European Union's sports programme, the initiative was designed to equalities-proof the tournament and make it more inclusive of the LGBT community. A Pride House – a safe space for LGBT people – had been initiated in the previous tournament, jointly hosted by Poland and Ukraine, but due to lack of support from the organisers and fearful of government crackdowns, the initiative had hardly been publicised, defeating the objective. With concern rising that Russia, as hosts of the next World Cup in 2018, were hardly very friendly when it came to accepting the visibility of their own LGBT community, this project was determined to set some standards that future mega-sporting events should live up to. The EUROS are the largest sporting event in the world after the Olympics and FIFA's World Cup.

My experience of the EUROS started as an armchair fan in 1972 when my favourite 'other' team, West Germany, demolished England in the quarter-final first leg match at Wembley 3-1. England held out for a goalless second leg, but the result just showed how far the Germans with their sweeper system had left behind England in the international rankings. Four years later it was Wales who qualified for the last eight, losing out to Yugoslavia. When the tournament finals were increased to encompass eight teams rather than just the semi-finals and final, England qualified in 1980. Hosted by Italy, the matches were tarred by hooliganism, and England inevitably faltered. We failed to qualify in 1984 and lost all our group stage matches in the 1988 tournament.

In 1992 I was speaking at a trades union conference in Bournemouth. As I got to the Winter Gardens by the seafront, I was disgusted to hear that 'Turnip Taylor', as our manager had been named by the tabloids, had substituted Spurs' Gary Lineker for the average Arsenal player Alan Smith. Graham Taylor had won not very much as a manager but had turned average sides into good ones by playing the long-ball game. I shall never forget my anger as I rose to speak that Taylor had substituted Alan Smith for Gary Lineker, who was just one goal away from equalling Bobby Charlton's all-time goal scoring record for England.

"Madam speaker, thanks for inviting me to Bournemouth," I said. "I know we all feel gutted with the General Election defeat [the Tories had defied all odds to win their fourth consecutive parliamentary election a few days before], but worse things have happened, such as the deplorable suggestion that Alan Smith is a better player than Gary Lineker. So as the Prime Minister's term will be limited, we can rejoice that so will be the tenure of Graham Taylor." It took another two years for the FA to get rid of Taylor and another five years to get a Labour Government. Thankfully all the delegates had been following the football and roundly applauded me, which is more than England deserved going out at the group stage once again.

In 1996, thirty years after that solitary World Cup win, football came home as England played host for the EUROS, now extended to 16 teams. After a shaky start with a draw against Switzerland, the norm for English teams in finals tournament, England beat the auld enemy Scotland and then trounced the Dutch with a master class from Shearer and Spurs' Teddy Sheringham. Again I was at a union conference in Bournemouth, but this time as a delegate. The win matched the *zeitgeist* of the age – Britain was climbing from a recession and was just one year away from a change in government. The hooliganism that had blighted our reputation in the 1980s and 90s seemed to be a thing of the past. When it came to the semi-final against a now united

Germany, both sets of supporters were singing the anthem for the tournament 'It's coming home.'

I watched the game with David, Vince and Fraser in North London. David was at that time seeing a German lad, Hans, and they had been wisely banished with Hans' German friends to a gay pub to watch the match for themselves. It was the most important match since England had beaten the Germans in 1966.Like that match, it went to extra-time, with both Darren Anderton and Paul Gascoigne missing chances to win the match, but unlike that game, it went to the sudden death of penalties. Despite beating Spain in the quarter-finals on penalties, the inevitable happened and we lost. Let's just say that the following trip to the pub to meet happy gay Germans celebrating wasn't the best end to the night. David ditched Hans the very next day. A case of 'auf wiedersehen pet'.

Concerned that hooliganism was rearing its head again, the Labour Government elected a year later took a different and more insightful tactic to combat the problem. Rather than the Tories' approach of banning matches and contemplating identity cards for supporters or withdrawing teams from future competitions, they actually worked with fans to isolate the extremists. After the violence of EURO 2000, resources were diverted to fans' embassies for the 2004 tournament in Portugal. These were run by fans for fans and provided independent advice, support and counselling for travelling supporters. They would also liaise with security officials before and after the match to work together on resolving safety problems. Together with banning orders for the worst offenders, this meant that the tournament re-established English fans' reputations. It also meant that I got a free pass to the last 16 England v Croatia match, as my friend Peter worked for the Foreign Office, which was working with fans. It was possibly my best experience watching England play. Wayne Rooney got a brace and England won 3-1. Unfortunately I missed our demise to the Portuguese in the quarter-final (again on penalties). The visit also gave me time to spend with my relatives, many of whom lived in Lisbon, and I also found a road named after me: Rua Telles!

The 'Wally with the Brolly' (the FA clearly hadn't learned lessons from past appointments) meant we didn't reach the 2008 tournament held jointly by Austria and Switzerland. I went to the fateful night at Wembley where we managed to pull back to 2-2 after being 2-0 down to Croatia in our last qualifying match, but lost eventually to another goal due to a goalkeeping error. To make it worse, the rain poured and poured that night, but Steve McClaren was all right – he had an umbrella and didn't do the honourable thing and resign after the loss but waited until he was sacked, so that he could get a massive handout from the FA as a severance payment for the rest of his contract. I knew what I wanted to sever of his that night! Croatia got their revenge that night for Portugal, but the silver lining in that cloud was that Spurs signed up Luka Modric and Vedran Corluka from the side that roundly beat England.

Four years later and a couple of managers on, Roy Hodgson took over for 2012. England followed a similar pattern, qualifying well but going out on penalties to a higher-ranked team, this time Italy in the quarter-finals. I met Roy, now 67, in Paris as we were about to enter the fans' embassies conference before EURO 2016. I blurted out "Nice to see a friendly face" and as all celebrities do when they fail to recognise someone they're not sure they know, he replied "Nice to see you again".

So from that fans' embassy initiated by England supporters 12 years ago, there were now 19 of the expanded 24 countries in the finals tournament who had similar embassies. Funded by UEFA as part of their Respect Fans programme, they gave support to FSE to organise them. It would be my job to train them on equalities and diversity issues.

However, the issue of hooliganism had been dwarfed by the issue of terrorism in the lead up to the tournament. Paris and Brussels had been the victims of a horrifying attack by Islamist gunmen who had killed132 people in random shootings on the streets of Paris on a November night which coincided with a friendly match against Germany in the Stade de France, the stadium that would be used for the final in July. The terrorists had shot and killed people at cafés, restaurants and in a music venue. They had tried to get into the ground and detonate bombs. As police searched for the gunmen who had escaped, it became apparent that they were part of a cell based in neighbouring Belgium. They would launch a deadly attack on the Brussels city airport, the same one I had travelled to earlier in the season to see Spurs play Anderlecht. On the morning of the attacks, I had flown out from Gatwick to Hamburg. Stadiums, restaurants, airports, clubs – it all showed that we were all potential random targets for bombers who were prepared to lose their lives, and for what? The mood was sombre when we gathered at the prestigious headquarters of the French Football Federation to launch the fans' embassies and call for volunteers. No wonder the day was dominated by security.

Towards the end of May we had recruited our volunteers, so I headed off to Paris for another weekend in a less salubrious location on the outskirts of the city. The volunteers had been recruited through Concordia, a social civic programme in France for 18-25 year olds to get experience of serving the community as interns. President Hollande had met the volunteers and an FSE colleague of mine who was responsible for the fans' embassies programme. It showed how seriously France was taking EURO 2016 as an attempt to rebuild its reputation as a safe, secure place to visit and do business. On my earlier visit, traders, taxi drivers, café owners had all said how business had suffered a severe downturn in the wake of the events in November. One of the immediate side-effects that I had noticed in that visit was that everyone was pleased to speak English, none of the much-vaunted French reluctance to anglicise their business environment.

The volunteers were a good cross-cultural section of young people in France and had varying degrees in their proficiency with the English language, but all outshone my failure to get even an O level in French. For all my parents' abilities to speak five languages (English, Swahili, Hindi, Portuguese and Konkani), I had barely mastered one. Actually I do myself a slight disservice, as FSE colleagues welcomed my pronunciation and articulation of the Queen's English. It would become a running joke of that weekend that I spoke with a BBC accent. The Brits within FSE were not easy for the other Europeans to understand – the main English supporter, Kevin Miles, who I had met whilst he chaired the Pride in Football event, spoke with a Geordie accent, and the Northern Ireland and Welsh lot spoke in a Celtic accent that had a speed of a supersonic jet. In fact when it came to the translation of their speeches, they found the English easily the most difficult to interpret because of their national and regional accents.

The weekend was disrupted by strike action. France had notoriously strong trades unions which had flexed their muscles under two previous presidents, Chirac and Sarkozy, who had both tried to moderate or weaken the legacy of their socialist predecessor, François Mitterrand. As I had liked the social democracy of the West Germans in the 1970s, I also admired the French Socialism of the 1980s. Mitterrand was a great counterbalance to the right-wing ravings of Thatcherism that we had to endure in the same decade. Much of what he had left after 14 years in office was, like Thatcher's legacy of 11 years in office in the UK, still intact. So the French still enjoyed generous welfare benefits, reasonable pensions and a 35-hour working week with strict regulation of employment practices. The incumbent president had proposed only slight relaxations, but this had led to massive protests, including picketing of oil depots, transport go-slows on trains and the Paris Metro, and riots and demonstrations in major cities. I had a sneaking liking for France; so they probably had a lower standard of living than us, maybe one less foreign holiday a year, but at least they knew that their children benefited from good resources when at school and they could look forward to a pension in their early 60s. One such benefit was that our cadre of volunteers received 500 euros a month from the government. Compared to our interns in the UK, who were lucky if their travel expenses to work were met, this seemed entirely reasonable and justified.

As in Belfast earlier in the season, I got slightly nervous before my speech, the presentation and hosting the event. In fact I would have been a bit worried if the adrenaline hadn't start pumping. In my case it hadn't done so for a long time. As I embarked on the first of three long weekends of travelling and talking ahead of the EUROS, a doctor's appointment at the hospital out-patients had given me cause for concern. Since falling victim to the sepsis infection I mentioned at the beginning of this memoir, I had been diagnosed with hypothyroidism. This meant that after a tumour in my pituitary gland had burst, something I didn't even know at the time, my body was failing to produce the necessary levels of thyroxine and testosterone that I needed to function. This had been addressed by a combination of tablets and a quarterly injection. Apparently one in 1,000 men suffer from this condition, which is much more prevalent in women, where it is commonly referred to as hormone replacement therapy or HRT. I had come off the injection last Easter as my testosterone level had climbed back to a normal production level. However the consultant said it was now back at a dangerously low level. That would explain the extreme tiredness and lethargy I had recently felt. Thanks to an administrative blunder it would take a further six weeks to get the injection I so desperately needed. In the meantime I had to just get up and get on with the taxing long weekends.

How do you get the interest of young French people when you're a tired 51-year-old Englishman? I just said: "I am gay, I have a disability and I'm an immigrant. How many of you thought I was all of that?" Let's just say that didn't need to be interpreted – they were hooked to find out more about my experiences watching football. And as I had found out with the anti-homophobia training I had done the previous year with the Spurs foundation course students, there was nothing I should have been worried or anxious about. I am always amazed at how tolerant, understanding and accepting this generation is of the need to appreciate diversity and respect equality. One of the fans' embassies supporters of a similar age to me had slipped into the volunteers' training. He took me aside and told me he had a gay son and a lesbian daughter and was so glad that I had brought up this subject. This was the first time he had the issue raised within the context of supporting football. So maybe the second day wouldn't be as hard as I had first imagined, as I would now have to face the fans – a range of supporters, of all ages, from Albania to Austria, Switzerland to Sweden and Belgium to Croatia.

I had been warned that the cultural nuances between supporters within countries were as important as the more obvious differences of race, religion, sexuality, disability or gender. I tried a different tack here and talked to them about realistic situations that they could face whilst hosting fans' embassies – what would they do if a woman fan said she had been harassed or a disabled fan couldn't access a stadium? By putting them in real situations which they might find, rather than lecturing them on theory, I got some great feedback and even a round of applause at the end. Even the man from the Russian FA decided to stay for the session and I got interviewed by the Russian contingent for a piece on You Tube.

I also got a much-needed understanding of how some supporters are trying valiantly to battle far-right extremism amongst their own fans, and how UEFA with its laws and match observers might actually be a hindrance. For example, their own guide to 'unacceptable' symbols includes the Russian flag pre-1918. Now as the flag of St George was seen previously as a symbol of racists and the far-right in the England of the 1970s, until we reclaimed it back, a similar turn of events has happened in Russia, but UEFA refuses to accept that things have moved on. Prevention is so much better than the iron fist of stadium closures, which penalise all fans, not only those deemed to be racist. Bans don't seem to work, as Croatian football has suffered a number of such bans, but they have failed to root out the far-right amongst them. Empowering other fans to be able to do that would be a much bigger step forward.

On the second weekend, with the tournament less than a week away, I returned to a very soggy Paris. In fact more than soggy – the ground was saturated, the Seine had risen to flood levels not seen in a generation and the strikes were getting more militant. We had planned this weekend as a network meeting for fans who were already anti-discrimination activists to look at challenging homophobia, but also the growing number of people coming to Europe seeking refuge from war.

The first day was devoted to a range of projects which integrated refugees and asylum-seekers into either playing or watching football or both. I was truly humbled as I recorded the details of the voluntary projects, many of which received very little funding from either the football authorities or the state. The problem had reached a new peak with the increasingly fractious civil war in Syria, which had displaced nearly two million people. Football supporters had in the main been welcoming, with banners saying 'Refugees Welcome' displayed by fans in the German Bundesliga for example. I know my brother was nearly moved to tears when he saw this, saying that similar displays of affection in the UK, when we migrated in the 1960s, would have meant so much. However there was a feeling that welcoming wasn't enough – we needed to make them feel that they belonged. So writers like myself could stop saying 'them', 'they' but rather 'us' and 'we'. It was good to hear from an Albanian refugee in Germany who said that the football project had literally saved his life. We became friends, even though he's a Woolwich fan!

The second day was spent preparing for the October international conference for LGBT fans against homophobia. With a healthy grant from the German Bundesliga and the funds from the Queering Football conference, this would be a week-long event in Berlin to celebrate the fifth anniversary of the Football Fans against Homophobia campaign, the annual meeting of Queer Football Fans and a day of international guests and speakers from the UK,USA and Mexico – the latter the country where FIFA has taken action against homophobic chanting – the first action of its kind. Who knows we might even get-together a worldwide LGBT football supporters' network, less than 30 years after the GFSN was formed in Britain.

With that positive thought, I headed back to London. It took me 14 hours – yes you've read that correctly, a journey that takes 40 minutes by plane took 14 hours door-to-door.

Trains literally on go slows and flights cancelled meant I landed at midnight at Luton Airport, fortunate enough to catch the last slow train to Gatwick where I was reunited with my car for the return journey to Brighton, arriving at 4.30am on Monday morning. What would the third weekend have in store, and could France cope?

The opening weekend of the EURO 2016 tournament arrived and I would be there for the opening of Pride House in Paris and celebratory events in the fan zone near the Eiffel Tower. Well, that was before the venue was flooded and the event had to be moved to the Saturday, the day after I left. At least the matches got under way on time with the hosts beating Romania at the Stade de France. My return plane was also on time – now brought forward to that night because the Pride House event had been postponed. So I was left struggling with a suitcase and another go slow which meant that instead of four trains an hour to the airport, you were fortunate to get one. Maybe the drivers wanted to see the opening match, and who could blame them. However, it did mean trains crushed to the roofs, though being a regular traveller on the worst rail line in this country, the London to Brighton route, this obviously came as second nature. Despite this, this stay was much more comfortable than the previous ones.

Sunshine had restored the smiles to the faces of weary Parisians the next time I was there and it was good to be back in the LGBT quarter of the city, Le Marias, for meetings of the Queering Football project team in the Paris LGBT centre. It was a pleasure to meet the organisers of Pride House, the French LGBT Sports Federation (FGSL) and to be invited by them to Marseille during the tournament to speak as one of a panel on the topic of homophobia and discrimination in sport. To cap it all we had also just confirmed a fan event before the England v Wales match in Lens, in neighbouring Lille, on Human Rights in sporting events with a range of speakers from the English Football Supporters Federation, the Russian supporters' group CSKA Fans against racism and Amnesty International and me. And because I was missing out on the re-arranged opening of the Pride House, I had been invited to the closure during the final weekend of the tournament.

We had battled against storms and strikes, and this was even before a ball had been kicked. However I looked forward to Lille, Marseille and then being reunited in Paris. What could go wrong?

Let the tournament begin!

CHAPTER 22

THREE CANCELLATIONS AND A COUP

✳

JUNE/JULY 2016

The plan for the Queering Football initiative was that we, FSE, would organise three fan-led events to discuss homophobia and our partners the FGSL, the French Gay and Lesbian Sports Federation, would organise three events with the LGBT community to discuss discrimination in sport.

Our first event was around the England v Wales match in Lens. The stadium in Lens was one of the smallest in the tournament and somehow the draw had conspired to place two of the best supported teams in a group match. Furthermore Lens couldn't cope with the thousands of fans expected to follow England and Wales, so most would be staying in Lille, the destination of the Eurostar train, and then travel to nearby Lens on the day for the actual game. The draw also put Russia in the same group and their first game against England would be in Marseilles. The city has history, as far as the conduct of English fans are concerned. The beach in the city was the scene of running battles between England supporters and local youths before the 1998 World Cup tie against Tunisia. Now added to the mix were the far-right Russian nationalists who had caused trouble four years earlier in Poland and Ukraine.

What transpired in the weekend before the match and after the game, including Russian fans storming English fans inside the stadium, was an unhealthy mix of organised brutality, over-reacting police using tear gas and drunken English fans not helping themselves. Now we had the prospect of English and Russian fans, some tanked up and a few tooled up, meeting again for the second round in Lille, the day of Russia's game against Slovenia and the day before England met the Welsh – all on the day of our proposed event. To make matters worse, the authorities were going to curtail drinking in both cities, which meant that meeting in a bar and trying to engage both Russian and English supporters in a discussion on human rights possibly wasn't quite the most safest thing we could be doing. Wisdom prevailed and we cancelled the meeting.

Fate had played its hand again and I had been denied a possible stage in Lille and the prospect of a ticket for the match in Lens the following day. England had, as always, made heavy weather of qualifying from their group. A draw against Russia in Marseilles allowing their opponents to score an equaliser in injury time had been followed up with a last-minute winner against Wales. Then a drab draw against Slovenia, where Hodgson had inexplicably rested our best players, including most of the Spurs contingent, had meant we qualified as runners-up. It seemed we would pay for this by having to meet our old adversaries Portugal in the second round. However, another last-minute goal (this was a peculiar pattern to the first-round group matches) meant that we faced Iceland, with a size of population the equivalent to the city of Leicester, in the last 16.

With some trepidation then, I would travel to Marseilles for the event organised by the FGSL. Surely nothing could go wrong here. It would be a day visit for an afternoon meeting in the fan zone on the beach. Temperatures soared to nearly 40 Centigrade in the preceding week. When I arrived at the venue I was happy to be welcomed by a near life-size impression of Justin Fashanu. Once again, not for the first time, I felt his hand to be on my shoulder. Justin was part of an exhibition put together by the European Gay and Lesbian Sports Federation of sporting LGBT icons.

The meeting would also be the day after the EU referendum. It was billed as the Prime Minister's attempt to keep a fractured Tory party together, and David Cameron had gambled on a vote on Great Britain's membership. It went badly wrong. A terrible campaign which played on people's fears misjudged the mood of those voting, who were not prepared to back the PM. The night before I had travelled to France, the UK decided by a small margin of

52% to 48% to pull out of the community of 27 nations. After spending the whole night watching the results come in, I arrived in Marseilles to be confronted by incredulity and wonderment as to why we had made such a decision, which would worsen our position economically. A week later I would reflect on these views as France overtook us as the fifth richest economy in the league tables after the value of sterling shrank to levels not known for 35 years.

The scene of the meeting was perfect; the French Riviera in bright sunshine and cloudless skies was an amazing backdrop, never bettered. I was also suitably impressed by the regeneration the quayside had undergone, ironically with EU Regional Development funding. What was different here from the many similar projects I had seen on the British mainland was that everywhere around the redevelopment sites the EU flag flew, so that local people could see at first-hand how EU membership had benefited the city. It was too late to do something similar to the vast swathes of Britain that had gained from EU funding but had voted decisively for Brexit, as we soon came to call it. I reminded myself of Swansea, which I had visited with Mum for our match last season that had been regenerated with funds from the same pot, but had voted against EU membership. I was very tired, having stayed up all night watching with growing incredulity as the referendum results were announced. It seemed we had voted to put a barbed wire fence around the island of Great Britain and slowly watch ourselves die from the resulting economic isolation.

The meeting itself was a damp squib. The organisers had advertised different times for the discussion and despite having access to the fan zone, an impeccable venue and with the Mayor's support, only half a dozen people turned up. I made the most of a poor meeting by talking about Brexit and promising that England would win the EURO tournament and that the Brexit vote would be overturned. "We will be back" I said in my best Churchillian voice, to much applause and hilarity. My flight was booked for the same evening, so I had some time to watch the football in a bar and have a tour of the port area of the city.

Calmly I said goodbye to my hosts and entered the departure lounge of the airport to hear –
wait for it – that my flight had been cancelled. This was turning into a repeating nightmare. I had no overnight clothes, the next flight was in three days' time and most vitally, I had none of my prescription tablets. Somewhat fortunately, there was an overnight flight going to Manchester and I managed to swap my tickets, flying into England at 2.30 the following morning. Missing a coach back to Gatwick, I spent an unwelcome and chilly night in the station. I arrived home in Brighton at 4.30 in the afternoon, exhausted. To make matters worse, I had left the day free to apply for a job with the closing date for applications the following day at midday. However, I was knackered and just couldn't face working on the application. I knew that my time with FSE was coming to an end, with my six-month contract finishing in July. The job I was applying for was just ten minutes away from where I lived. I managed to crawl out of bed the following morning and completed the application at 11.59 with a minute to spare before the closing time.

England went lamely out of the tournament, losing 2-1 to minnows Iceland. Adding to the feeling of isolation caused by the Brexit decision, I felt that Great Britain had become Little England in less than a week.

The second of our fan-led events was a collaboration with the National Association of Football Supporters in France at St Etienne. I didn't go, as the conference was going to be entirely in French, and we would contribute to a workshop on anti-discrimination initiatives. I was pleased to hear that links had been made with some LGBT French football fans keen to establish links with others in Europe.

Unfortunately, our last event fell by the wayside. Before the Germany v Poland game we wanted to hold an exhibition on discrimination in the fan zone. However, security concerns over a possible clash between the two sets of supporters scuppered this event, much to our consternation. The display would be seen later in the tournament in Paris, as the Germans qualified through to a semi-final match against hosts France.

France qualified for the final and would meet Portugal in the final at St Denis on the Sunday of the first weekend in July. There would be one final discussion panel hosted by the Mayor's Office in the Paris fan zone outside the City Hall, the majestic Place de Ville. The event was better attended than the one in Marseille and the sun shone down on us that weekend. It all looked as if France, after all the difficulties it had faced in a high summer of inclement weather, industrial action and the scare of terrorist attacks, would finally benefit by winning the trophy for the second time. As ever, I tried to get some of the glory, as Portugal suddenly became my second team.

As I entered the Pride House in Paris that night to watch the final, I became a new minority, the one supporting the underdogs. There was a noble ceremony of closing the Pride House by handing the baton to the Russians, hosts for the 2018 World Cup. The final wasn't the best of matches but it did have its fair share of drama and excitement. It was goalless and seemed to be drifting to the inevitable penalty shoot-out to decide the winners. I decided to walk back to my hotel to soak up some of the Parisian atmosphere. I knew that it would be loud and brash if France went onto win and on my return walk, I found fans huddled around Parisian cafés and restaurants, all in good spirits and the triumphant chord of 'Allez les Bleus' being sung relentlessly. I only saw one Portuguese flag on that return journey and as I went to speak to the fan with it, something quite extraordinary happened; Portugal, at that very minute, scored and the flag was hosted above grieving French supporters. It proved to be the only goal of the game, the winning one, for against expectations Portugal had won EURO 2016, their first-ever international trophy.

Despite the inclement weather which spasmodically affected the tournament, the over-zealousness of some of the policing and the early fracas with Russian far-right elements, the tournament had been far better than we had feared. The involvement of 24 teams as opposed to 16 hadn't reduced the quality of the football played and in fact the debut of teams like Wales, who went all the way to the semi-finals before losing to the eventual winners, made it one to remember. From my point of view though, England's woeful dismissal at the hands of Iceland, the failure to engage with fans on the subject of tackling homophobia and the awful result of the referendum left a bad taste in my mouth. However, this was tempered by the surprise of an invitation to be interviewed for that job I had applied for with a minute to spare.

It had all begun in Belfast a year before and it would end in Izmir next week. I had decided to pack in my job just before Belfast and hadn't regretted it since, and now a year later, I had an interview for the senior management position at a local charity, fortunately for me on the day before I travelled to Turkey.

The Turkish city on the Mediterranean Sea was the venue of the FSE annual summer meeting. Hundreds of fans from all over Europe were expected from at least 16 different countries. There had been some rumblings of discontent that Turkey was chosen as the venue due to the ongoing problems of bombing campaigns from Kurdish insurgents and Islamist terrorists. However Izmir hadn't been the scene of any such atrocities and I looked forward to spending some quality time with fellow fans in which would be the last event working for FSE.

As I arrived a day early for the network meeting, I reflected on my time with FSE. Yes, it had had some highlights, but most of the time, unfortunately, had been spent in airport departure lounges – I now knew every inch of Charles De Gaulle airport in Paris, for instance. I hadn't seen one football match and if I am entirely honest I wondered what had been the impact on Queering Football.

The first day of the conference went well. Held in a modern auditorium and with many Turkish fans volunteering, issues such as membership schemes, stadium bans and supporter control of clubs were well received. The hospitality was, as always when Turkish people are involved, warm and welcoming. I made many new friends, regaling many with fictional 1}1}accounts of English hooliganism.

As I was returning to my hotel and looking forward to the second day, I was alerted by social media that something was happening in Istanbul. Worried that it might be another bombing, I took small comfort from the fact that we were hundreds of miles away. As the night unfolded and I began to get dozens of messages on Facebook, I realised that a coup was in progress. Elements of the military had attacked the Turkish parliament and were engaged in combat with government supporters in Istanbul. I was told that the airport in Izmir had closed and we would have to stay in our rooms, as a military curfew was in place. This was not turning out the way I had planned. There was an eerie, dark and ominous silence in what was usually a busy street outside.

As the night went on, the air was punctuated by cries and cheers of support for the government, as the Turkish President had asked his supporters to come out on the streets to demonstrate their support and there were many klaxons hooting and sirens wailing to confirm this.

We awoke in the morning to a confused situation. It seemed that the government had defeated the coup and was now rounding up its opponents. In Izmir there was hardly anyone on the streets, and assemblies were outlawed. In these circumstances, the conference had been cancelled. I changed my flight and flew back on the overnight plane to London as soon as the airport had been reopened. I had got the last available seat on the plane, and this time, the flight wasn't cancelled.

I arrived home to be told I had got the job.

CHAPTER 23

COMING OUT ON AWAY DAYS

✹

AUGUST 2016

The start of the 2016-17 season felt like one in the early 1970s. These were the days before Liverpool was going to dominate the League and before the advent of the Premiership where three teams – Manchester United, Woolwich and Chelsea – stood head and shoulders above the rest. This had all changed with Leicester City winning the title last season. I felt that now at least seven teams could justifiably claim to have eyes on lifting the trophy in May. Both Manchester clubs, a rejuvenated Liverpool, ourselves, the Gooners and the Foxes as holders, could each put forward a reasonable case for becoming champions. My favourites were Chelsea, though without any European football and with a new manager, I thought they would prove to be just out of reach of the rest of the 'Magnificent Seven.'

Our season started away at Everton. There was a time when wherever we played, we would all make the effort to travel to see the opening match. It all began with the start of the Premiership breakaway from the Football League in 1992. Our first match in the new set-up was away at the Dell to Southampton and we stayed the weekend in nearby Bournemouth. After Brighton and Blackpool, the south coast resort was known for its modest but busy gay scene. Although we could only draw 0-0 with the Saints, our weekend was made a little more memorable by a visit to the Bolts gay nightclub to see one of the first ever appearances of a band destined for fame – Take That.

One of the most notable away outings was to Sheffield Wednesday at the beginning of the 1994-95 campaign. Spurs had splashed out the cash to capture World Cup stars Ilie Dimitrescu and Gica Popescu from Romania, who had made the last eight of the summer's tournament in the USA. It is fair to say however that their signings were not on the same scale as 14 years earlier, when Spurs bought World Cup winners from Argentina – Ossie Ardiles and team mate Ricky Villa. Ardiles was now Spurs manager and after a poor first season, where at times a frail Spurs defence toyed with the possibility of relegation, Ossie had been given another chance to lift the team. Certainly another pre-season signing from the World Cup seemed to show the scale of the club's ambition: the German Jurgen Klinsmann.

It was therefore with much anticipation that we travelled to Hillsborough to see what the new team could do. As I mentioned previously, as an England supporter, I wasn't the first in line to praise the signing of Klinsmann. He had after all a reputation for diving and wouldn't win any plaudits for sportsmanship.

The match was still easily the most memorable away day opening fixture of the past 25 seasons. Spurs came top in a seven-goal thriller, with Klinsmann scoring a winner and celebrating in some style with a choreographed celebration where nearly half the team dived on the pitch. Still immersed in our win, we spent the best part of an hour trying to recall where we had parked the car. When eventually we did get to it, we were just in time to escape some aggrieved Wednesday fans who weren't too happy to see Spurs fans still in their manor. We decided to go to the nearest gay pub for a post-match celebration, only to find it packed to the rafters with Spurs fans. It didn't take long for it to dawn on us that these weren't dozens of more potential GFSN members but they had stumbled in here as it was the nearest to the station. Unfortunately, not everyone could accept that it was a gay pub and some of the comments on the various leaflets and papers in the pub were uncalled for.

Determined however not to let it spoil our day, we got our drinks and settled down to discuss the astonishing win. The team would get the Enid Blyton tag of the Famous Five, not because we defended like five-year-olds, though we did, but because Ossie chose to play with five attackers up front and in midfield: Anderton, Barmby, Sheringham, Klinsmann and Dimitrescu.

The scoreline wasn't the only thing that would stay in the memory. Because it had taken us over an hour after the match to get to this watering hole, tucked away in the corner of the pub was a first-team player who had also probably taken the same amount of time. He was instantly recognisable as Ian Walker, our goalkeeper, with three very tough-looking minders. Astonished and wondering if he was waiting for the first train back to London or like us was on a gay lads' weekend in Sheffield, we racked our brains to think why an England international player had decided to drink in a pub, let alone a gay one. Would there be a revelation in a sleazy Sunday newspaper as a result we wondered? When Walker and his chums decided to join in some of the anti-gay 'banter', these thoughts soon dissipated. We should have known better – he couldn't be gay, he was wearing a shiny shell suit and no gay man worth his salt would be seen in one.

Once the train for London arrived, the pub soon emptied, leaving ours the only occupied table. The bartender turned round rather suspiciously when we asked him where the next gay pub was we could drink in. The fact that he thought it slightly weird that we were real football fans was unfortunately an easy assumption to make of the LGBT community. We had regularly been asked to leave some pubs in Manchester's gay village which didn't allow football fans entry, as however camp our protestations, they just didn't believe there were such things as genuine LGBT football fans.

Talking of being camp reminds me of the previous season's opening day fixture against Newcastle United at St James's Park in the 1993-94 season. Newcastle would be the team we would aspire to be in the 1990s. We knew we didn't have the money to follow the big four of Chelsea, Arsenal and the likes of Liverpool and Manchester United. We thought the best we might be able to reach was the odd cup win, a larger stadium and the occasional season in Europe. It would take a decade for at least two of those aspirations to be realised. Newcastle had a stadium to be proud of with a 50,000 plus capacity and despite its location, not being in the multi-cultural city of London, it managed to attract foreign stars. The simple fact was that we were outbid by them for several key players, as they could play higher wages.

I travelled to Newcastle for the weekend along with David, Fraser and Vince. We dropped in on David's parents, who didn't know he was gay. We won the game with a solitary goal from Teddy Sheringham and went on the gay scene to celebrate. When we were collected by a minicab driver from our guest house, he was really surprised that the four of us in Spurs shirts wanted to be taken to a gay club. In perfect Geordie he said "Are you sure lads? Are you gays?" As a result, and on every away trip since, we spend much time and get great joy asking ourselves in broad Geordie accents, 'Are you gays?'

On this visit, we actually should have had a coming-out party for David. When his dad phoned him to see if we had returned safely to London, he said "Do you have something to tell me, son?"

"Not particularly", was the nervous reply.

"It's just that we found one of your friends rather camp – not that there's anything against that," his father said in turn.

After a sigh of relief, David came out to his parents, who were not surprised, and they all lived happily ever after. By the way, David never did ask his dad which of us was camp!

We went on several trips to Newcastle over time. Once we went into the largest gay club in the city, which had just opened a cloakroom. The attendant looked despondent but was soon glad to see us as we were some of the first to drop off our jackets. Despite it being midwinter, most Geordies, including the gay ones, decide to go clubbing in short-sleeved shirts or mini-skirts. The attendant told us that the cloakroom had only just opened, as they never thought they needed one. However, given that not many clubbers seemed to be using it, he was scared of losing his job. What a difference from the large queues in most London venues.

That night I was glad to score with a couple, one of whom turned out to be Chris Hughton's accountant, and we spent the night in their home, in the suitably named Park Lane. Of course years later Hughton would become Newcastle's manager.

David's brother Peter was a season ticket holder at St James's Park and he ventured down to London to see the Toon play at White Hart Lane one season. After the match he had to catch his train back up north and we dropped him off at King's Cross, only to find that his train had been delayed. We used the time to take Peter to a nearby gay bar, Central Station. The bar had now become home for our GFSN Socials and these proved to be so popular that the manager had turned his upstairs bar into a sports venue with satellite television, allowing us to watch games together. This may seem a minor thing to mention but there wasn't a gay venue in London in those days that even thought it had to cater to LGBT football fans – quite the opposite in fact.

As we settled down to our drinks in the sports bar we noticed that we weren't the only ones there – on the next table was a bespectacled man dressed only in a raincoat and happily masturbating. We didn't know where to look, let alone what to say. Peter must have thought this happened at every gay pub in London, as he stayed silent supping his pint. After an awkward frisson of silence, it was David who first asked the barman what was happening. He said their customer who was a regular had thought it was a sex night and he didn't think of challenging him as he was, until we entered, the only customer there. So whilst I was telling Peter that this didn't usually happen, Fraser and Vince then began a discourse with David, saying he should have left the man alone as he wasn't doing any harm. We did however agree to relocate to the downstairs bar and decided to leave the discussion on whether it was legitimate to complain to another day.

At the opening of the 1996-97 season we were away at Blackburn Rovers. They had actually done a Leicester by unexpectedly winning the Premiership a few seasons earlier. We spent the weekend in Blackpool, renowned for its gay scene. Saturday night was spent in one of the town's many gay clubs celebrating a two-nil win courtesy of two goals from Chris Armstrong. David was born in Blackpool and in his childhood was a keen Seasiders' supporter. During the time we were in the club, he thought one of the clubbers sitting on the next table looked familiar and then he realised that he was a doppelgänger for Stanley

Matthews, one of the best English players of the 1950s. He had the bottle to ask him, and the man turned out to be the great player's cousin.

I also have to attribute a Spurs football match for outing me. In the 1978-79 season we reached the quarter-finals of the FA Cup. We replayed the tie, after a 1-1 draw at White Hart Lane, at Old Trafford, on a midweek night in March. Despite playing well, we went out 2-0 to the eventual runners-up that year, Manchester United. In those days, there was no live coverage of the FA Cup, except for the final in May. You had to watch highlights on programmes such as the BBC's Sportsnight to catch up on how your team had fared. Let's just say that I calmed my nerves before watching the programme that evening, not knowing the result, by taking a break with the gay magazine *Zipper*. With no internet access, boys of my age accessed pornography by picking up magazines from the top shelves of newsagents. For me however, it wasn't *Fiesta* that caught my eye. Usually I would delve into the delights of *Zipper* magazine in my bedroom. This month's edition was a special delight, as it had an Eddie Kidd lookalike dressed in a football strip, well not fully dressed, but I expect you can use your own imagination to fill in the rest. I was slightly late in coming, and could hear the strains of what still remains my favourite television theme music of *Sportsnight*, from the lounge downstairs.

In my rush I forgot to hide the magazine. A few minutes later as we were knocked out of the cup, my mum was also knocked out to find a gay porn magazine on my bed. Some lame excuse was given, such as I had found the magazine and was simply curious, but I had been outed after watching Spurs play football, just a few months from reaching the age of 14.

Spurs drew 1-1 with Everton, beat Crystal Palace 1-0 at home and tied 1-1 with Liverpool, also at the Lane, in our first three league games in August.

CHAPTER 24

OUR MAN IN MOSCOW

✸

SEPTEMBER 2016

At the end of a tepid August, interest off the Premiership field was raised by the Champions League draw at UEFA's headquarters in Switzerland. For the first time in six seasons, Spurs entered the hat. Well actually it wasn't a hat but an elaborate ball, which Ian Rush found terribly difficult in opening. The Welsh striker was there as the final would be held in Cardiff's Millennium Stadium. Last time round, in 2010, we had had to endure a qualifying round in Berne with Young Boys in the Wankdorf Stadium: there is a whole comedy farce in that one sentence, to which I have already alluded, but the best ones are worth repeating again.

This season we went through to the group stage and on paper, we had the luck of being drawn against none of the fancied clubs. The opponents we had to overcome were familiar to us in the guise of Bayer Leverkusen from Germany and AS Monaco from the French Ligue, both teams we had encountered in previous seasons of the Europa League. Neither of those clubs appealed to me for a visit. There would be little chance of getting a ticket to see Spurs on the French Riviera as Monaco's ground only had a small capacity.

It was the top seed in the group, however, which really drew my attention. CSKA Moscow, probably the easiest of the seeded teams, would be our first opponents away. Moscow was a city I had long aspired to visit. As a teenager, at the height of the Cold War in the early 1980s after the then Soviet Union's (USSR) invasion of neighbouring Afghanistan, there would be nightly reports from a BBC news correspondent outside the Kremlin. Red Square was definitely on the top of my bucket list. The USSR had blown apart at the end of that decade and had been replaced by a looser federation, or commonwealth, of independent states. Mother Russia had emerged and communism had been defeated. In the intervening thirty years, however, Russia's political history had toyed with bankruptcy in the 1990s to the establishment of an oligarchy in the 21st century, which had fully embraced capitalism with the creation of an affluent middle class and extremes of poverty and wealth. Now Russia seemed to be reasserting its power as a rival to the USA, and many were beginning to write about a new

Cold War. Russia had allowed former Soviet satellite states such as Estonia and East European allies like Poland to join the West, firstly through becoming members of the European Union and then also of the defence alliance, NATO. This had left Russia with an ever-decreasing border between itself and what seemed to them an all all-powerful West. A resurgent nationalism had transformed Russia, so that when a new government in neighbouring Ukraine applied for EU membership, many Russians within the country and those in their native home of Russia thought that was a step too far. Russia had retaken the Crimea from the Ukraine and had also retaliated against western influence in Georgia by supporting regions such as Azbakhia to unilaterally declare allegiance to Moscow.

One of the friends I had met in Belfast and who had supported my application to join the staff of FSE was himself a refugee from those Georgian wars and had now settled in Moscow. We had both said that if CSKA, his team, drew Spurs in the Champions League, I would have to visit him in his apartment in Moscow. As soon as the draw was made I really had no option but to book a flight after being invited to spend a week in the capital city. Just a year before, the thought of travelling to Moscow to visit the places I had seen on the television so frequently in my childhood, would have been unheard of. The reason was a state-led clampdown on gay rights. The Communist regime had always viewed homosexuality as a Western deviancy and an offshoot of bourgeois decadence. When the USSR was dismantled in the early 1990s, the laws were liberalised and the LGBT community had begun to climb out of the closet. All that had changed with right-wing nationalist mayors of cities, and then Putin as President linking LGBT lifestyles to paedophilia and promoting legislation that effectively told the gay community to go back indoors. Pride marches were routinely disrupted by the authorities, who turned a blind eye to the open harassment and abuse of the LGBT community in Russia. This had reached fever pitch when Russia was chosen to host the 2018 World Cup. With liberalisation in the West for gay lifestyles culminating in the acceptance of civil partnerships and even equal marriage in some countries, the Russian authorities' clampdown seemed extreme and medieval in comparison. I had joined calls for FIFA to consider withdrawal of Russia's eligibility to host the next World Cup tournament.

That view had changed after talking to people like Robert Ustian, the CSKA fan from Moscow. He had established a supporters' group to campaign against racism on and off the pitch in Russia. It worked tirelessly with club officials, team players and supporters to combat the prevalence of racist chanting in games. They insisted that if Russia were permitted to hold the World Cup, this would give them an extraordinary opportunity to embrace diversity. I had also met campaigners form the Russian LGBT Sports Federation in the EURO Pride House in Paris earlier this year, who were making the same case. My views began to change – isolation just leads to antagonism and the stigmatisation of the LGBT community in Russia. For some, the thought of an official Proud Lilywhites trip to Moscow seemed to be a step too far, but I wanted to see for myself.

Before I turned my attention to getting a visa for my Russian trip, there was a whole host of matches. Prominent amongst them was our season debut at Wembley. With rebuilding of our stadium proceeding at a quickening pace, we had transferred our 'home' for Champions League matches to the national stadium. AS Monaco would be our first opponents. Last season we had stormed to a 4-1 victory against the Ligue 1 opponents. However, with a new manager and a couple of new signings, the French team were now a different proposition. On a glorious late summer evening I arrived to what felt like a dream – at Wembley with no opposition fans. The stadium was filled with 80,000 fans, with only a few hundred of them supporting the 'away' side. It was surreal to be at Wembley with no opposition support and for the entire stadium to be filled with Spurs supporters. However, it was real, for the match attendance broke all records – the highest for a Spurs home match, the most at a Champions League tie. Never before had so many supporters attended a Spurs match outside a final, home or away, and I was one of those fans.

Before the match, the absence of opposing fans around the stadium was as strange as the full-on smiles of the Spurs supporters, delighted to be there. I could get used to this, I thought, and might have to next season, when our ground was finally closed and all our home matches might move to Wembley.

If history was made off the pitch, it certainly wasn't on the turf. For the fifth game in succession, Spurs lost at Wembley, a record which was one short of our dour c1}1}onsecutive FA Cup semi-final losses. We started the match in low gear and were twice caught short at the back as Monaco raced to a two-nil lead by half-time. We did improve in the second half though, with Harry Kane scoring – and he missed a sitter to leave us pointless. There were lessons to be learnt then as we went to Russia, particularly for our defence, and another loss would make qualifying to the knock-out stage very difficult.

Arriving in Moscow, I was taken by Robert on a tour of the metro system. Yes, you've read that right – a tour, because the metro system is a bit like travelling in an art gallery. The brilliance of each station is marked by magnificent chandeliers, brilliant frescoes and amazing murals. I had been told of this in advance by friends who had travelled to the city on the first leg of the tourist trail, which eventually ended up at St Petersburg. I was also told by others, including my brother, that the Muscovites were unfriendly people who never smiled; that the food was poor; the climate cold and basically the city was stuck in some medieval time warp. Nothing – I was to find – could be further from the truth.

So it did help having Robert with me, who was a delightful and enthusiastic host. And why not? If I were a guide hosting foreigners on a trip to London, I would be extremely proud of my home city. Both Robert and I had faced similar difficulties. We had both experienced having to assimilate to new locations early in our childhood and both had an affinity with patriotism. Robert and I would have political discussions where he berated the West and I was left defending British foreign policy. I had been more than a bit miffed at having to pay nearly £100 for a visa, spending half a day filling in forms, four times incorrectly. However Robert shamed me with his story of getting a visa to visit the UK. Not only was the cost extortionate, he had to endure an interview with baffling questions being asked by British Embassy staff.

Robert, as I have said, speaks perfect English, and as we travelled around the city, either by tram or in the metro, we spoke all the time. At times I was aware of people listening and some even intervened. One said how great it was to see someone from England and added that if I had time, I would be most welcome to travel to his home republic – or, has he proudly asserted, Soviet state – of Belarus. I had listened earnestly as he spoke, convinced that he was berating me, but as Robert informed me, the Russians were very polite and the absence of a smile was due to a cultural tendency to see smilers as fools. Food wasn't a problem either. The self-service canteens in the shopping arcades were a delight to eat in, and not just for their intricate architecture. I never went hungry or had any recurrence of my stomach problems. Moscow is a modern, bustling European city with all the brand names you would find in any capital within the continent. I felt that going there had opened up my eyes and I could make judgements based on what I had seen and experienced for myself.

I had also been told that the match would be played in a hostile environment with the small contingent of Spurs supporters surrounded and harassed by gangs of neo-Nazis. Well only one of those predictions came true on the night.

The week before in Moscow had been marred by bad weather, a mixture of gloomy skies and heavy rain. However, I was fortunate that despite for a few drizzles, most of the time I spent there was bright, sunny and mild. On the day of the match itself, Robert received a phone call from BT Sport. He was known as an expert on Russian football and had the added extra of not needing to be interpreted. They wanted to interview him before the match, so we arrived at the new CSKA Arena early that morning.

The stadium was brand new, with a capacity like that of the existing White Hart Lane. Robert said the interview would be a good opportunity to raise the profile of his campaign against discrimination and counter what he believed to be the propaganda of British TV programmes like BBC3's *Extreme Russia*, which highlighted what he thought were misconceptions about Russian attitudes towards people of colour, migrants and the gay community. Considering that I fell into all three categories I was a little concerned at Robert's insistence that I should wear my Proud Lilywhites T-shirt below my jumper, just in case he could persuade BT Sport to include me in the interview.

In fact it turned out that the reporter was keen on keeping to his original brief and only interviewing Robert about the club's history. However, he did sense our disappointment, and to counter this he decided to invite us into the ground. Delighted to be invited, I was 'over the moon' to see that the interview would take place next to the pitch! What an opportunity, I thought, as I sat in the dugouts that would that evening seat Mauricio Pochettino and his coaching staff.

As the interview closed, we asked one of the ground staff to take a picture. Again as on the tram the previous day, I was a bit concerned at the discussion Robert was having with the non-smiling Russian. Was he displeased at my T-shirt emblazoned with the rainbow flag? I hesitated as he pointed to me. Then he pointed again, and being a bit shell shocked I didn't hear Robert's assertion that we should get behind the pitch-side advertising. I looked towards where he was pointing and saw the UEFA Respect banner. He wanted us to stand there, as he knew exactly what we wanted to portray and he had no qualms about it. Respect to the Russians – those I had met had been nothing but kind and friendly, if a bit reserved, not much different from those at home, I thought.

So there was I on the pitch behind a Respect banner wearing the rainbow flag in the middle of so-called homophobic Moscow – out and proud to be here in the Russian capital city.

The match itself lived up to my expectations. It couldn't have been more different to our first game as it was the smallest Tottenham contingent I had been with at a game – numbering only a few hundred. What a contrast to the largest home attendance at Wembley. The police presence was heavy but not unduly so, and there was no sniff of any hooliganism or any racist chanting from the home fans. In the second half as Spurs continued to dominate after taking a lead, the fans in the home end stripped to show many welcoming, manly bare chests. Was I really here or was this another late-night dream, I wondered? As for the match on the pitch, we held onto our lead to gain three valuable points and our first win in this season's competition. Rainbow T shirts on the pitch and near-naked men in the terraces – who said Russia was homophobic?

Outside the Champions League, it was a really good month for Spurs with a 4-0 away win against Stoke City (the same scoreline as last season), a 1-0 win at the Lane against

Sunderland followed by a 2-1 win at Middlesbrough, all in the Premiership. We also convincingly beat Gillingham as we started the League Cup with a 5-0 home win.

CHAPTER 25

BETWEEN BERLIN AND BRIGHTON

✳

OCTOBER 2016

Football Pride Week, held in Berlin, was the centrepiece of the Queering Football initiative I was involved with whilst at FSE. It was the first time, other than the Manchester Conference in 2014, that LGBT fan clubs from around the continent had got together. For me that was a problem: got together for what? What had we achieved from Manchester and what did we want to achieve from Berlin? It was with some reluctance, therefore, that I accepted an invitation to attend.

Although I had left FSE in the early stages of the planning for the event, I had proposed that the T in LGBT actually meant something and that we should invite Sophie Cook. I had met Sophie in Eastbourne earlier in the year, during an event at the University of Brighton's site in Eastbourne, where we had both spoken on a panel about our experiences of homophobia in football. Sophie had been born a man, had got married and had children. Then, following a career as an RAF pilot, she had decided to change her gender. She had announced this to a packed dressing room at Premiership side AFC Bournemouth, where she was the team photographer. They and the club had supported her throughout her transformation. Now she had become an icon for those in the game who wanted to make football more open to people from the trans communities. She had moved to Hove, where she hosted her own show, 'Beyond the Rainbow', on the Latest TV channel, the community channel for the city.

Arriving tired and dishevelled in Berlin on a cold Thursday night after a full day's work at my new job, I heard that although Sophie had been invited as a guest, she was not down to speak in the opening plenary. I later realised that some of this was due to German hostility; as one put it 'The English always believe they are the only ones who know the best when tackling discrimination'. I was slightly taken aback by this, and it was with some trepidation that I entered the conference venue on Friday morning. The previous day had been held entirely in German and funded by the German FA with club officials meeting with QFF, the predominantly German alliance of queer football fan clubs, on how they could tackle discrimination in the Bundesliga.

Friday would bring together all LGBT fan clubs invited from across Europe and it would be held in English. The opening plenary discussion involved UEFA and a representative from each of the conference organising groups, FSE, QFF and Football Fans Against Homophobia, the German and Scandinavian equivalent of Football v Homophobia. I immediately raised my concern that yet again the T in LGBT was invisible, and was told that as there were no trans members within the three organisations, the panel was as it was. For some reason this didn't stop a guest from the USA being invited to be part of the panel. Despite Sophie being someone who actually worked with a Premiership club meeting footballers almost as a weekly occurrence, it was not deemed necessary for her to speak.

The discussion centred on one major grievance from EURO 2016. During the tournament, Football Fans Against Homophobia were not allowed to bring in the rainbow flag to matches. UEFA were adamant that this was caught under its regulation of banning the display of 'political' symbols during matches. So much for our aim in Queering Football if we weren't even allowed to show how inclusive fans, both straight or otherwise, wanted the tournament to be. And surely UEFA's own campaign with banners such as 'No to Racism' were political messages. To much applause I derided UEFA's position as untenable, saying that in the UK the rainbow flag was proudly displayed throughout several Premiership games, including that of the Proud

Lilywhites in one corner of the ground. The discussion was prescient in the light of events the following month, when FIFA banned England and Scotland from wearing armbands displaying the poppy during their World Cup Qualifier, which coincided with Armistice Day. Wales and Northern Ireland were also penalised for 'allowing' supporters to display poppies.

The trip to Berlin had come just one week from my extended visit to Moscow and with my poor health, I had had no time to recover. In between Spurs had outplayed Manchester City at the Lane, but due to lethargy and now having to work during the day, I hadn't managed to get down to North London to watch it. It rounded off an invigorating September for Spurs, and despite an injury to Harry Kane, the South Korean Heung-Min Son had filled the gap with five goals and he became the first Asian player to win the Player of the Month award in the Premiership. It looked good for us, even if I felt a bit disjointed.

My misgivings for what the Berlin event would actually produce was emphasised by the workshops held on Friday afternoon. These were exactly the same as those held in Manchester two years before, where I had first met colleagues from FSE. They were about organising LGBT fan clubs; developing international links; tacking discrimination and our approach to the next two FIFA World Cups in Russia and Qatar. It had the feel of those trades union conferences I used to attend twenty-odd years ago – the same people at a different venue talking about the same issues and not really moving the agenda on. Twenty years previously I could accept these, as there was always the pleasure of socialising in the evening. Now in my fifties and at times feeling ten years older than that, I had become more cynical and wearisome.

I skipped Saturday's deliberations to do some sightseeing. I had visited Berlin for the first time at the end of an exhausting inter-rail trip in 1991 with David, just two years after the Wall between East and West had fallen down and less than a year after the Federal Republic in the West and the Democratic Republic in the East had been united. Now Berlin had completely transformed itself, with vast areas regenerated including the German Federal Parliament, the Bundestag, renovated, and with the move of the country's capital from Bonn, this had spurred a renaissance to the city. It was like visiting something new. In the middle of a tour I was swept aside by a peace demonstration which took me to the new memorial to the Holocaust and also gave me a chance to pay respects to the LGBT victims of the Nazis.

So if I left Berlin on Sunday fairly disappointed in football terms, some of my still lethargic feelings had been mitigated by the vibrant feeling of the city and its inhabitants.

Returning to Brighton, I had my first really important meeting in my new job, the Annual General Meeting. Much of the preliminary work had already been done with an annual report produced in a calendar styled format, invitations sent to all the important dignitaries and the venue and food booked. However, I couldn't help a feeling at the back of my mind that something was missing: I didn't feel I was totally engaged with the job. Although I had decided to take a backseat role at least until my six month probationary period was over, I sensed that my absences both in Moscow and Berlin had generated a sense of suspicion by some staff members. Maybe I was just looking for pessimistic points to dwell on when none were apparent. I had found in my first two months, after more than 18 months without a full-time job, that the rigour of making meetings was somewhat exhausting, especially evening meetings, which took their toll the following morning. However, I felt sure that given time, things would improve.

On the day of the AGM I had appeared on the local radio station Juice FM to explain what our organisation did and how people could get involved in our work. Later that afternoon Sophie Cook interviewed me for LatestTV ahead of the meeting that evening. I went home to prepare my speech and get more formally attired. I wanted to use the occasion of my speech to make the well-established organisation a bit more outward looking. For me, it felt as if it was resting on its laurels and the granting of three-year funding from the local city council and health service, just before I joined, would give us an opportunity to reflect on where we wanted to be by 2020. I wanted the charity to be run more by its members, turning supporters into activists and seeking fresh blood on both the trustee board and within the office staff. I was the first CEO that the organisation had appointed from outside and I would use the meeting to set out my stall and a vision for 2020.

And then it all went wrong. Whilst getting changed for the meeting, I realised I had lost my wallet. Not a problem, I initially thought, I would just retrace my steps, as I had plenty of time to make the start of the meeting. Slowly but surely however, the hunt for my missing wallet descended into a farce. Driving around like a madman, I went back to work, to where I had had lunch, to the shops I had visited on the way back home, but there was no sign of it and my breathing and heart rate were now aggravated. Then suddenly, with only 30 minutes to go to the start of the meeting, I realised that I had no time to park the car at home and travel by bus to the venue for the meeting, or at least that's what I thought. My drive to the venue was like the journey from hell. The clock kept ticking and when I finally crawled through rush-hour traffic, there was nowhere to park near to the venue.

I spent at least ten minutes trying to park, and then as I got out of the car I almost fell over. Fortunately two Good Samaritans accompanied me to the venue. Arriving with just five minutes to go, I collapsed, shaking and crying inconsolably. My speech became slurred and an ambulance was called. Suddenly my world had been turned head over heels.

I was taken to the local accident and emergency ward and after a brain scan and blood tests, the diagnosis was a severe panic attack and not something more serious, such as a haemorrhage or even a stroke. More rest was needed, and time off work. It wasn't the perfect start to the perfect job. However I continued to enjoy the job, despite at times finding the pace hard to keep up with. Though with retrospect, it shouldn't have been a surprise when the Chairman of the Board's charity, the man who had given me the job, said that he had received a delegation from the rest of management team criticising my work ethic and commitment to the role. However, in terms straight out of the football world, he said the Board of Trustees had all faith in my ability; they had appointed me to the role and would like me to continue. After a sleepless night, the parallel sounded more than familiar.

I rang him the next morning and said that although I welcomed the Board's vote of confidence, it had left me feeling as if I was between a rock and a hard place. I decided that it would be impossible for me to continue as manager, if the team around me had stopped playing for me.

It was a pretty dour month on the field as well, a drab 1-1 draw against WBA was followed by another nil all draw at Bayer Leverkusen in the Champions League. A draw against Bournemouth away meant that a win at home to reigning Champions Leicester City, was essential to reinvigorate our League campaign.

CHAPTER 26

OUT OF AFRICA

✳

NOVEMBER 2016

So just a couple of days before November began, we faced the reigning Premiership champions, Leicester City, at the Lane. Arriving early, I was slightly disappointed to receive some hostile banter from the away supporters, a couple of whom pointed to their badges, which said 'Champions', and loudly declared that this was something I'd never see. Not a good start, and not one I was accustomed to with Leicester fans – maybe their recent elevation had gone to their heads. I nobly stuck to my routine, not attempting to give that comment a reply, and headed for the Spurs megastore. Entering the shop was usually a first port of call before having brunch, and today I was especially early and pleased to see that 1991 FA Cup legends David Howells and Paul Allen were signing autographs.

The shop is routinely full of fans, especially the many international visitors our club seems to attract. Over the years this has fluctuated between a significant Scandinavian contingent, to Germans when we had World Cup winners Steffen Freund and Christian Zieger and from further abroad such as the USA with goalkeepers such as Brad Friedel and Casey Keller on our books. Steffen Freund was a legend at Spurs, even though he had never scored for us, or maybe because of this. I wasn't too sold on him – but then who was I to say, I had never taken to Gareth Bale when he was a full-back or Harry Kane after he had returned from being on loan at Millwall and looked slovenly.

As the saying goes however, never judge someone until you actually meet them. And how true that is. In November 2014, I actually met Steffen, who volunteered to referee a game between the Proud Lilywhites and Gay Gooners to mark a year since our birth. He was a lovely guy and made us all feel welcome. I still have the shirt he signed for me on that day and he even bought us all a drink. He said that it was a delight to referee the match, and that in Germany being gay wasn't an issue.

At one time in the Spurs shop I bumped into a group of Italians, and in amongst them was one-time Spurs player Paulo Tramezzani. I say one-time because he probably only played for us properly one time! He was a fullback bought by Christian Gross at the start of the 1998-99 season, apparently only on the basis of a video he had seen of the player. And there he was in the middle of dozens of Spurs supporters, going totally unnoticed by both customers and staff and purchasing items in the shop. When I told one of the staff that they had just sold a product to an actual team player, he didn't seem that bothered. To be fair, neither was Tramezzani; in the two seasons he was on our books, he only played seven times.

Today my eyes were immediately attracted to an African man in the store wearing a Kenyan cricket shirt. Amongst our pre-season signings was the defensive midfielder Victor Wanyama, who had rejoined Pochettino at the Lane from where they first met at Southampton. It was the first time I could say that Spurs had a player born in the same country that I was, for over 50 years ago, I was born in Nairobi, Kenya's capital, and I spent the first four years of my life totally oblivious to England, football and Spurs.

The wearer of that shirt turned out to be a Martin Chege, who was there on a busman's holiday. He was a freelance sports journalist back in Nairobi and had spent the past fortnight visiting some of our famous football venues – Wembley, Old Trafford and even Woolwich. He'd left the best until last, coming to the Lane as a proud supporter of Wanyama. He was intrigued that I had been born a year after Kenya's independence but couldn't speak a word of the official language, Swahili. His English, it goes without saying, was impeccable.

We immediately hit it off and I asked him what side of the ground he was sitting in. That's when his smile turned to a frown. He had found it impossible to secure a ticket, but had come here to soak in the pre-match atmosphere. He had recently become a parent for the first time and was busy getting a load of baby wear from the shop. He had no idea who David Howells was, as he was born just a year before the last time we won the FA Cup Final, but he still got him to sign his new Spurs baseball cap.

As we said goodbye, it dawned on me that there was a possible way he could get a ticket and not from the touts outside the shop, who were asking hundreds of pounds. I asked him if he had his press pass and he showed it to me. I thought he might just have a chance of getting into the press gallery to see the match. I rang the Head of Supporters Services, not expecting him to pick up my call before such an important game, but he did. I had known Jonathan Waite, who was the Supporters' Liaison Officer (SLO), since being co-chair of the Proud Lilywhites two seasons before. He had been excellent in assisting me to arrange the fan group's first public meeting in the Bill Nicholson suite in September 2014 and was this season nominated for the best SLO in the Premiership in the annual Football Supporters Awards, for the third season running. He kindly told me to go to the match day reception, use his name and see if Martin could be accommodated. So off we trekked to Lilywhites House. They in turn told us to go to the West Stand where the match day office was and they in turn told us to go the North Stand, where the press office was.

Well at least it gave me an opportunity to take Martin on a tour of the new stadium, which was rapidly being built around the existing stadia. By Christmas we were told the outer shell would be complete, with the next year seeing the demolition of the stadium and the filling out of the new one.

Chris, a Ghanaian, was a very helpful steward and he showed us to the press office. I had long suspected, almost correctly, that most West Africans supported the other side at Woolwich. Not Chris. He was Tottenham born and bred, but as he said to Martin and me, like us he was 'Out of Africa'.

The press office was ram-packed and they said to come back at 2pm to see if a place was available. With an hour to kill I took Martin for somewhere to eat. As we ate our lunchtime meal, we struck up an immediate rapport. He told me about his background, saying his ethnicity was Kikuyu and that his next assignment as a sports reporter would be the Africa Cup Nations in Gabon later in the season. He was intrigued at my Kenyan heritage and had heard of the events that had led to my family and thousands of other East African Asians leaving Kenya.

The circumstances of 1968 are now known as the 'Exodus'. In comparison to the deportation enforced four years later in Uganda by the ruthless dictator Idi Amin, Kenya's transition from colonisation to independent republic was less severe. However, events in Britain and Enoch Powell's notorious 'rivers of blood' speech would change all that. Kenya was slowly but surely introducing a policy of Africanisation of the civil service, where many middle managers, like my own father, had held positions. So if Dad wanted to stay, he would have had to renounce his British passport and take up Kenyan citizenship. He sacrificed a relatively high standard of living to decide to come to Britain, where he thought we, my brother and I, would benefit from an English education, as he put it. It was a decision that would change my life and ruin his. For as the time came nearer to depart, the Labour Government in Britain was reeling from the local election results that year that showed that in many of its urban heartlands, their usual white working-class voters were deserting them in droves for the Conservatives, resentful of Commonwealth immigration. Talk was growing that the Home Secretary, James Callaghan, was contemplating removing British nationality from East African Asians, including my family, who had been recruited from India. Such a decision would make us stateless and as many pointed out, was racist, as no such bar would be placed on white Canadians, Australians or New Zealanders travelling and settling down in the UK.

In a panic many people, including my family, rushed to get to the British mainland. In a frenzy, Dad sold his house and our commodities and resigned from his job. Mum came first, just in case legislation allowed only those with dependants already in the UK to follow. It was, all and all, a traumatic time. Dad sold his VW car and instead borrowed what could only be described as an old banger to drive us to the airport. On the way, excited to be going on a plane for the first time, I carelessly pushed my brother. The door hadn't been locked properly and we both tumbled out onto a major roundabout. The memories of us falling out of the car are still very vivid for me, all these years later. I can still see the eyes of the driver of a Mini who skidded closed to me – white as a sheet, as pale as his skin, in the heat of the city. He had been inches away from running me over.

Those last few days clearly affected my father and led to his breakdown two years later when he was sectioned, spending three months in an institution. It would wreck what was left of his life as spent much of the remaining 25 years of his life heavily sedated, a shadow of his former exuberant self. However, as I was to learn much later, it was not just this experience that had weakened my father. There was a much more shocking episode, when he had just turned 21 in 1953. His mum, my grandmother, who I would never meet, was murdered in her own home, and my Dad blamed himself for not being by her side. The youngest of six children, he was his mother's favourite and always used to go home for lunch from work. On that day he didn't, and while he wasn't there, she was murdered, hacked to death with a machete, a victim of the Mau Mau uprising for independence. In the early 1950s there was no such thing as bereavement counselling or therapy; Dad was just expected to get on with life.

Martin was clearly affected by my story, and he explained that he had lost family during the rebellion. The colonial authorities had interned many Kenyan people simply because they supported independence and held them in what amounted to war camps, where many were treated to torture and abuse. The survivors, who are dwindling every year, are still litigating for reparations a generation later.

We returned to the Press Office, and it was now past the intended time of 2pm. We were told that even if we had got there in time, Martin wouldn't have been successful in gaining a seat in the gallery as the match against the League Champions was too much of a draw for the press. I turned to him, my disappointment clearly showing. He embraced me and said he didn't mind. The day was already a success, he informed me. I looked at him quizzically, and then he told me that he had met me, had been taken on an impromptu tour and then had realised that our close affinity and shared background had meant that he had received something better than being able to attend the match.

I looked at him quizzically. "Because I have met you, Darryl – a friend for life," he said. I smiled and felt warm.

In amongst the crowd of 36,000 that regularly attend games at White Hart Lane there must be so many things, other than supporting Spurs, that two people have in common with each other. You never know who you will meet, and however difficult a day may be at first, it always has a chance of getting better. I could have chosen not to speak to Martin, especially after my disappointment with those Leicester City fans only a few moments earlier. I am glad I didn't.

When I returned home after the match, I told Mum of my story of how I had met a fellow Kenyan at Spurs and how he was a Kikuyu. Mum knew many Kikuyus from her years in Kenya. She had worked, laughed and lived with many and was shocked when Dad told her that his mother's murderer was from the same ethnic group. Maybe, just maybe after all those years, my grandmother could now rest in peace, knowing that the goodness of future generations, coping with the consequences of shattering events, had broken a new, if unlikely friendship – and this all because we went to the same football match, thousands of miles from where we were born and where she is laid to rest.

The match itself was highly entertaining and followed much of the pattern of our crucial league encounter last season. We had all the possession but were unable to turn our chances into goals, although this time we did score, only for Leicester to equalise shortly after and hold on for the draw. Considering that City had had such a bad start to the season away from home, it was definitely two points lost. The Foxes had played much better in their Champions League group and looked likely to qualify for the second round knockout stage.

Meanwhile we had another 'no-show' at Wembley playing awfully to Bayer Leverkusen, losing 1-0. Three League games in London saw us draw with Woolwich 1-1 and narrowly beat West Ham at home 3-2 with two late goals, one a penalty from a rejuvenated Harry Kane. Kane scored another penalty at Stamford Bridge as despite dominating the first half and taking the lead, we eventually lost 2-1. A few days earlier we had crashed out of the Champions League, losing 2-1 to AS Monaco away, again Kane scoring from the spot. So within a week, our brief sojourn into the elite European competition was over and we had lost our unbeaten record in the Premiership.

And just for the record and at the third time of being nominated, Tottenham Hotspur's Jonathan Waite deservedly gained recognition as he was awarded Supporters Liaison Officer of the Year

CHAPTER 27

WEMBLEY WOE

✳

DECEMBER 2016

When I first started supporting Spurs the history and traditions of the club were ingrained in me, particularly the fact that it had never lost a match at Wembley Stadium. We were unbeaten in the FA Cup after seven final appearances before losing to Coventry City in 1987 and unbeaten in any League Cup Final until losing to Liverpool in 1982. Well we certainly made of up for that extraordinary record with some very ordinary appearances in our last run of games at what might become our home stadium, whilst the building works continue at White Hart Lane1}1}.

So as we approached our last Champions League match against CSKA Moscow, it was important to register a win to stop the rot of six successive losses at Wembley. The first of those was in 2009 when, as I related earlier, we lost rather unluckily, I thought, to Manchester United in the League Cup final. We were thwarted by a really impressive performance by Ben Foster, the United goalkeeper. I subsequently believed that he should have played more matches for England and was certainly underrated and undervalued. With the match goalless it went to penalties, and we lost 4-1. The result meant that we had lost our first match in the League Cup competition since losing the semi-final against the Gooners in 2007.

A year later we played Portsmouth, who have now tumbled to the fourth tier of professional football, in the FA Cup semi-final. We were favourites to win, yet our performance didn't deserve that billing. We failed to live up to expectations on the day and lost our fifth consecutive semi-final in the FA Cup 2-0, again after extra time. The first goal was after an error from Michael Dawson, who never looked comfortable in his time with us without Ledley King next to him, and the second by our former player Kevin Prince-Boateng from the penalty spot. It was just desserts for Portsmouth, given that Harry Redknapp, our manager at the time, had left the club for us. Portsmouth lost to Chelsea in the final and at least we could say that saved us the prospect of meeting the Blues and contemplating losing our 100% record against them in Cup Finals and Wembley appearances.

That record would be tested again two years later when we played the West Londoners, again in the FA Cup semi-final. I have said enough about that dreadful appearance already; I have tried and failed to banish that 5-1 mauling from my memory. Until we are able to exact revenge against them at a similar level, despite the 5-3 win on New Year's Day 2015 in the Premiership, I won't rest easy. Again one of our centre-backs let us down in the 90 minutes and this time it was Ledley King, who was clearly not match fit, just as Darren Anderton shouldn't have played against Everton in the 1995 semi-final at Elland Road. We played Chelsea again, as I've already said, in the League Cup Final last year, losing 2-0.

And then to the Champions League. Two consecutive losses this season to Monaco and Bayer Leverkusen, despite two record home attendances, meant we really needed a win against the Russians. We had already beaten them in Moscow and they came into the match lacking in confidence. Apparently they had overstretched themselves in terms of finances in building the new CSKA Arena and had to let many squad players go for financial reasons. Added to this was the announcement of the departure of their head coach– this would be their last match with him at the helm – and the last before their winter break.

Before the match I met Elena Popova and her family from Moscow. I had first met Elena at the FSE training I had undertaken in Paris for the EUROS and we had become good friends. Unfortunately the Russian FA had failed to pay for her part in the Russian fans embassy, so she hadn't actually made the trip to France during the summer. As a wheelchair user, she had costs that couldn't be met and it was a shame she hadn't turned up. However, as she was the first to point out, neither had the Russian team! She had also had an interview for a job working for CAFE, the Centre for Accessible Football in Europe, which operates from offices at Wembley Stadium. I think we had developed an affinity, as she appreciates the battle against homophobia, as I support her campaigning for disabled fans. Although I was a tad disappointed to hear that she was a Chelsea fan and that she was going to their match on the following weekend, this at least reinforced my belief that I am correct in using the term Chelski to describe the Blues.

Despite giving the lead to CSKA against the run of play, with sloppy defending from Dier who was again a makeshift centre-back in the prolonged absence of Toby Alderweireld due to injury, we did run out winners 3-1 and should have scored more. The match wasn't without significance as we qualified as seeds for the Europa League round of 32 and I was glad when the club announced that those games, starting with the Belgian club Gent in February, would be played at Wembley. We needed to get into a winning run at the Stadium before next season.

As we left the Champions League competition, I felt that we had missed a golden opportunity. Our group was easier than the one we qualified from in 2010-11 to the knockout stage and gone as far as the last eight. I couldn't help feeling that Pochettino's decision to rest key players for the Monaco game away had backfired on him as it had done when he did the same against Borussia Dortmund in the Europa League last season.

In the Premiership we were back to form with a convincing

5-0 win at the Lane against Swansea – whose performance was the worst I had seen by an away team this season. We also won our other home matches against Hull 4-1 and Burnley 2-1. The only black spot was a narrow 1-0 defeat to Manchester United at Old Trafford. Then, unlike most Christmases, there was a 10-day break before we played Southampton away and won 4-1. The Burnley game was the most memorable for me as before the match in the Spurs mega store, I met Chris Wanyama, Victor's brother, who was in the UK with his family for Christmas. At least it wasn't another 'cousin'!

CHAPTER 28

BEATING THE BLUES

✳

JANUARY 2017

A New Year always brings new hopes, but in purely football terms it's only the middle of the season. Chelsea, without the onus of European football, had raced away at the top of the Premiership. Thirteen consecutive wins meant they had equalled Woolwich's record. Their one opportunity to go further than the Gooners would be against us at the Lane in our first match of 2017. Sometimes football is as real as theatre, you couldn't write a better script for this encounter. Our home record against the Blues, as I've previously mentioned, has significantly improved since the days Blues fans used to berate us with the chant, 'Can we play you every week?' Terry again steadfastly refused to see me before the match, as the last time we met, two seasons ago, Chelsea went on to lose 5-3.

There have been many times when I've witnessed bizarre score lines, both home and away. One comeback that stays in the mind was in the FA Cup in a fifth round replay in 1995 when we were 2-0 down to Southampton at their old ground the Dell before a stunning second half performance, including a hat-trick from Ronny 'the rocket' Rosenthal, saw us win 6-2. The buzz as a fan you get from those scores is matched by the depression endured after, for example, being 3-0 up to Manchester United in the League before losing 5-3. Topsy turvy doesn't come close to describing the emotions I felt on that day or the night when 3-0 up, at home against Manchester City in the League Cup and with one of their players sent-off at half-time, we still managed to lose the match 5-3. I had vivid nightmares, that night and for several after, of Ledley King crying in my arms.

So at times, the less convincing the scoreline, the better I feel I can cope with the emotions. We annihilated Chelsea that night and the 2-0 win doesn't come close to how we dominated the game through the full 90 minutes of the match. We were never going to lose that game as soon as the team entered the pitch and despite a five-minute storm from the Blues at the start of the second half, the performance, for me, was the best I had seen at the Lane all season. It's not always been like that with us against the Blues, as I have outlined in a previous chapter. If Chelsea were now the presumptive champions, we had given them two tough matches in the Premiership this season, going ahead at Stamford Bridge, before unluckily losing, and then winning the home encounter.

Terry doesn't like coming to the Lane. Not only because we both go into purdah in terms of our communications before and after the match, but also in his view, the atmosphere is like a cauldron and Chelsea fans feel the pressure we put them under. I have at one match seen horses being ridden into crowds to separate the two sets of fans before the match. On that occasion, David was lucky not to be trampled. Other than that one time, as I don't have to walk the gauntlet back to Seven Sisters tube station, about a mile away, I have very rarely witnessed any hooliganism.

That wasn't the situation when we played West Ham in the mid-1990s. In those days we used to drink in the 703 club, which is a raucous supporters' club annexed to the Tottenham Community Sports Centre in the High Road. We had won the game and had taken longer to celebrate than usual. About a couple of hours after the match, we heard a window being broken and the sound of Hammers supporters baying at us from outside. David and Vince escaped to the toilets, leaving me to deal with a couple of Spurs fans who shouted, "Where are your mates going? They're not running away are they?" I spluttered a faint 'No' and then witnessed his mate take off his beanie hat and wrap a couple of snooker balls in it. He looked at me as if I had to be ready to fight.

Fortunately there was an immediate sound of police sirens as the police arrived to deal with the West Ham supporters outside. Scott was the name of the lad with the snooker balls, and when Vince and David finally reappeared from their elongated toilet stop, he came over to speak to us. "Don't mind him, he's my brother," he said. "You're the queer Spurs lot aren't you?"

After gasping and choking on our beer, we said yes, and after another round of drinks Scott came out to us. He spent a long time telling us of his predicament. His brother and family didn't know he was gay and he had just left his girlfriend, who had found out. He was desperate to see the young son they had had together.

Over time Scott became one of our group, coming over to drink with us after games after his brother and his straight friends had left the 703 club. On one away trip to Elland Road in the FA Cup semi-final in 1995 against Everton, he joined us after the match to go on the gay scene. However, he was always looking over his shoulder, frightened that he might run into his older brother. Over the next season Scott came out to his family and although his Mum took it in her stride, he was physically abused by his brother. Later Scott was to become a partner of one of the owners of a gay pub we met together in London, even becoming a minor drag artist. From the Lane to the stage in high heels, he was finally able to be himself. Unfortunately, it also meant that he couldn't face going to the football any more, an experience he associated with violence, abuse and trouble.

Another Blues team, Cardiff City, also has a reputation for trouble amongst a segment of its supporters. When we played Cardiff in 2007 in an FA Cup third round tie at Ninian Park, Fraser and I went to the Welsh capital for the weekend. We drew 0-0 and after coming out of the ground, we were escorted – Europa League style – all the way back to the city centre. On each street corner however, this didn't stop the Welsh fans throwing bottles and coins at us. When we arrived at the railway station, where the Spurs fans were catching their trains back to London, we were more than a little relieved to see our hotel nearby. At this stage however, we hadn't been allowed to return to the hotel, due to the mindset of the police. They simply didn't believe our protestations that we were booked into the hotel and were content to kettle me and Fraser with all the other Spurs fans in the station. This was bizarre, so in the campiest voice possible I went up to the police inspector and said, "Do you really think we're a threat to the Cardiff fans, we just want to go clubbing?" He looked at me quizzically and then after much consultation decided that one of the police officers could escort us to our hotel. I did invite the 'escort' in for a drink, but I don't think he saw the funny side of my remark!

At the replay, I arrived at the Lane to witness police dressed in riot gear and the shutters down on all shops and cafés in the High Street. I had just leased a new car from work and a policeman came over to me advising me not to leave it parked in Lordship Lane as Cardiff City fans were fighting with us in the nearby Bruce Grove Park and were likely to smash cars on their way to the ground.

After the Chelsea win, we were up against Manchester City at the Eithiad. We had also beaten them 2-0 at the reverse fixture at the Lane earlier in the season, so we were quite confident of getting a favourable result. David and Fraser joined me to watch the game in a student pub in Brighton. Despite a fight at half time between two rival fans, we enjoyed the match as much as we could. Spurs were very lucky that night. Having gone down 2-0 to two soft City goals, after uncharacteristic mistakes from Hugo Lloris in our goal, we managed to equalise and when the final whistle went, it felt as if we had won the game.

Next we played another team in Blue, this time the League Two side Wycombe Wanderers, at home, in the fourth round of the FA Cup. And that match was like being on a roller-coaster. We had got our Tottenham back – the Spurs side who let in soft goals, showed no bottle and needed to be booed at half time. Pochettino rested nine first team players and we paid the price, going 2-0 down before a bizarre second half left the final score 4-3 to us. If this was to be our last cup tie at the Lane before the new stadium was built; at least we had won, but only just!

In our last Premiership games of the month we drew 0-0 with Sunderland away and beat Middlesbrough at home. We were now second in the league, nine points behind Chelsea.

CHAPTER 29

TONY BLAIR SAVED MY LIFE

✳

JANUARY 2017

I dislike February with the intensity that animal rights protesters conjure up for fox hunters. It seems I can always mark a week off in that month, flu jab or no flu jab, laid up with man flu. February is cold, cloudy and largely forgettable and one year it nearly saw me lose my life.

In 1994 I was responsible for putting together a conference for the European Year Against Racism in central London, where the keynote speaker would be the Shadow Home Secretary, Tony Blair. Tony was destined, along with

Gordon Brown, to be the praetorian guard of New Labour when the party finally came to power three years later. Blair was due to speak at the end of the conference and was delayed, due to a combination of bad weather, a poor train service and his last meeting overrunning its schedule. This had created some irritation, both with delegates and me as one of the organisers.

Still in the youth of my second decade, I was still, how shall I put this, getting my end away, or more delicately, having a fair modicum of sexual experiences. In a diary I kept at the time, in an attempt to keep pace with my sexual contacts, I would keep a tally of such encounters. Not one day would pass without such an occasion. Whether it was meeting up with a casual friend, defined as 'fuck buddies' or cruising the Heath, cottaging or clubbing, the diary shows that in the month of February alone, I had time for 28 such encounters. I still had time for engaging in lewd acts in cinemas as well. I was still up for Soho at weekends when we weren't playing at home.

With the dawn of satellite television in 1989 and the cable takeover of terrestrial coverage of the top flight of football, matches were moved from Saturday at 3pm to Sunday afternoons, Monday evenings and even on some occasions, Friday nights. Waiting for Blair, I had such an opportunity planned for Saturday afternoon, and I don't mean the football. Our league game at Stamford Bridge had been moved to Sunday, so I had planned to visit a sex cinema on the preceding afternoon. Yet Tony's lateness had put an end to that plan for fun. Maybe it was because he knew what I was planning to do and as a devout Christian he was revolted by the idea, or most probably it was his because his train to London was delayed by snow, that he turned up at 4.45 at our Westminster venue, rather than an hour earlier.

I had now begun going to cinemas outside the exclusive zone of Soho and many unlicensed ones had popped up elsewhere. One such location was in Farringdon, known as City Fantasy Club, with its sister venue at the Angel unsurprisingly named Fantasy 2. For a fiver you could pay for membership for a week and visit both when the fancy took you. Now City Fantasy's most popular time was after 4 and before it closed up at 6. My plan was that the conference would end by fourish and I'd be in situ at 5pm to have an hour of fun.

That's not how it turned out, and I thank Tony Blair for that. It was way past 5.15 when I shook his hand, thanked him for coming and decided to go home, realising that I wouldn't arrive at Farringdon until after the cinema had closed. Cursing my luck, I arrived home and switched on the television, where they were covering a fire in central London. Typical BBC News, I said to myself, why does a fire in London merit national headlines? Then I looked again and it dawned on me – six people had died in the blaze and more had been seriously injured jumping to escape it. The fire had torn through the building quickly and as an unlicensed venue, it had no proper fire escapes or precautions in place.

Then I realised that the fire had struck at the very place and at the exact time I had planned to be there. An irate customer who was drunk and had been refused entry to the City Fantasy sex cinema had returned with petrol and shoved it through the entrance door's letterbox, setting it alight. I had escaped by the fateful chance of Tony Blair being late for my conference.

I was so shocked that I could have been there that I had a very uneasy night's sleep and couldn't face going to the match the following day. We played well, going into a 2-0 lead, but eventually lost 4-3. Having access to cable TV gives modern-day fans the option of not going to matches, and this was the first time I did so.

The fire led to a crackdown on the emergence of these unlicensed premises by environmental health officers from local authorities and also by the police, who raided a few of them unannounced. It seemed that the police weren't just there to ensure the safety of the customers but were also using undercover detectives to arrest them for engaging in lewd acts. They were not in uniform and were acting as *agents provocateurs.*

One such police officer nicked the television commentator Gerald Sinstadt at the Fantasy 2 sex cinema in the Angel. He was prosecuted and found guilty for nothing more than having a bit of fun. Now I have to confess that the said commentator is one of my heroes. He started off his television career on ITV and was now a reporter for the BBC. What elevates him in my eyes is not just frequenting the same establishment as me, but more significantly being the first football commentator to call out the racist treatment black players endured during matches. Whilst the BBC's John Motson and Barry Davies would later claim that they couldn't hear any racist chanting or that it was all just light-hearted fun, Sinstadt had memorably 'left the field disgusted' at the baying of the West Bromwich Albion's threesome of Cyrille Regis, Lawrie

Cunningham and Brendan Batson after the Albion had won at Old Trafford 5-3 in a League match against Manchester United in 1978, the same year I had done the same at Chelsea after George Berry had been victimised.

Years later I would see Gerald Sinstadt sprawled out in the front seat of his car sleeping before a game at the Lane. I wished I had been able to thanks him for both his stand against racism and being wrongly arrested under draconian anti-gay legislation which should have been left behind in the Victorian era.

Tottenham Hotspur's Bill Nicholson suite was the venue for the launch of the Football v Homophobia (FvH) month of action. Just three years before the club had launched the Pride Lilywhites during the month, a year later we had 'come out' by leafleting supporters as they attended the match against Woolwich and last year the team wore the FvH T-shirts on the pitch preparing for the match at the Eithad. The only qualm I had was that the speakers for the launch, Donna from the club, Simone Pound from the PFA and Chris of the Proud Lilywhites, were all people I had heard from before. It would have been nice to hear support from one of our players. Little wonder then that the launch didn't make the press.

The month ended with the premiere of *Wonderkid*, a film about a gay football player struggling with homophobia on and off the pitch on Sky Sports. I was delighted that I got a totally undeserved credit on the film for the use of the new Spurs training ground. Unlike the play, the feature film with Russell Tovey seemed more realistic despite being only half an hour long. Someone somewhere should give a prize

to the endurance of Rhys Chapman in making an initial idea
a reality.

*Sandwiched in between two home Premiership wins against
Middlesbrough 1-0 and Stoke City 4-0, Spurs exited the
Europa League losing the tie against Gent 3-2 on aggregate
with a 1-0 loss away followed by a 2-2 draw at Wembley,
where Dele Alli was sent-off. We also lost to Liverpool in a
league match at Anfield 2-0. We beat Fulham convincingly
3-0 in the FA Cup in the fifth round to set up a quarter-final
tie against Millwall.*

CHAPTER 30

THE MADDENING CROWD

✳

MARCH 2017

Millwall are my favourite League One side, as are Brighton and Hove in the Championship, with Barnet getting my attention in League Two. Of course this doesn't mean I have any divided loyalties if any of these teams meet the Spurs, as all of them have had some connection with me in my life. Barnet is the nearest club to my childhood home in Finchley, whilst I now live in Hove. And as has been noted, I worked with Millwall whilst with Southwark Council and am still helping them with a research project on their Black supporters.

Millwall's Community Scheme and that of the supporters' equalities trust, Millwall for All, as I've said previously, have done some amazing work in the past few years to detoxify the brand usually associated with the club – that of hooliganism. Their catchy song is 'We are Millwall, No one loves us, we don't care.' The New Den, Millwall's home venue, is located just a short walk from where I worked in Bermondsey. The club's traditional working-class support derives from that neighbourhood, even though the ground is actually located just over the neighbouring border and inside Lewisham.

I didn't have a good time working for Lewisham when I joined the Council in 1997 as their Equalities Manager. The Council was taken over by New Labour acolytes after the local elections in May 1998 and began immediately to disband their equalities structure in pursuit of doing away with any left-wing stigma the administration had acquired in the previous era. At one stage, the incoming leadership even thought of changing the council's name to New Lewisham. The furthest they got was introducing an elected mayor for the borough, which put massive power in the hands of one individual. This season the council had tried to compulsorily purchase the area around the New Den, which would have meant the closure of the much-vaunted community scheme. Fortunately *The Guardian* newspaper had exposed dubious connections between the councillors making decisions and the private developers who wanted to regenerate the neighbourhood. This has now led to a temporary reprieve for the Lions.

So the anticipation was high when we drew them at the quarter-final stage of the FA Cup. They had reached the

2001 final and the semi-finals in 2014. This season they had already beaten the League Champions, Leicester City, in the last round. So on paper at least, they were going to be no pushovers. Pochettino had learnt from his previous mistake in the fourth round when he played a weakened side against Wycombe Wanderers and we won, if only just, by selecting a stronger team on this occasion. As it turned out we didn't need it, as we romped home to a 6-0 win. It would be a fitting end to FA Cup ties in our old stadium. Heung-Min Son scored a hat-trick and the only poor mark was that Harry Kane, who used to play on loan at Millwall early in his career, limped off with a nasty ankle injury after only playing the first few minutes.

Throughout the match it was clear that a large contingent of the Millwall fans had been chanting something every time Son got the ball. At half-time some of the supporters thought it was 'cheat', but we failed to recognise why Son had warranted such a slur. Others thought that the crowd were being overtly racist by using the term 'chink'. To be fair, Spurs fans were also guilty of singing inappropriate chants, calling Millwall 'pikeys' because of the history of the club's support from the Irish travellers' community and the location of a travellers' site near South Bermondsey, the nearest overground station to the stadium. After the game it became clear that Millwall were shouting 'DVD' every time Son had the ball, belittling his South East Asian origins. If the abuse had been down to only a few individuals, then the stewards might have been able to identify the perpetrators, but this was a large section of the 3,000 opposition supporters. If it was designed to put the South Korean off his game, then it did exactly the opposite, as his three goals proved.

In August 2011, a week after the Tottenham riots, Fraser and David took me on a legend's stadium tour of White Hart Lane for my birthday. Because of the disturbances where a crowd had burned down several buildings on the adjacent High Road, many people cancelled their places on the tour, leaving only the three of us, so we had the legend for that day, Garry Brooke, to ourselves. Garry was a player I saw when I first started coming to the Lane in the 1980s and was a used substitute in both the 1981 and 1982 FA Cup finals. Unfortunately, his career had been cut short after a serious car accident. When I told him my brother was a Chelsea season ticket holder, he asked me to remind him that the Blues have no history and had bought themselves silverware in the last 15 years. He was also critical of Millwall fans and told me that when he played at the Old Den and had to take corners for Spurs, he was regularly sworn at and abused by the fans. When this happened for the umpteenth time, he decided to turn round to his abusers and give them a taste of their own medicine, only to find that his main tormentor was a woman who was well beyond retirement age.

Millwall and Bermondsey have an unhealthy and unhelpful reputation for racism. In many respects this is unfair, and when I started working in the area I had to work hard, as I've already noted, on issues around celebrating St George's Day, where we made some great advances. However, the neighbourhood had suffered, or some might say benefited from, its historic insularity. Due to a 'sons and daughters' policy which limited access to employment in the nearby dockyards and provision of council housing to those with family ties in the area, the vicinity has largely been isolated to the growth of a multi-racial city in nearby neighbourhoods such as Peckham. In many respects, the Old Kent Road acts a white/black barrier between the two. Yet as we all know by looking at the Monopoly board, the lowest-priced property, the Old Kent Road, is one of the most deprived areas in London. Certainly low rates of mortality, poor educational achievement and low household incomes are features of the neighbourhood and this has led to the 'them and us' attitude that pervades the chants of their football club.

Having said all of this, my eleven years working in Bermondsey was probably my best experience in working within local government. When I first started, those I met were in the main really hospitable. That's not to say that I didn't experience racism. On one occasion a car drove over to where I was walking, asking for directions, the window was rolled down and I was told, "Fuck off, I won't take directions from a Paki." On another, as I was dressed in Edwardian costume and just about to launch a visitor guide to Bermondsey outside the venue for the press launch, the old Bryant and May matches factory, someone shouted, "Get lost you nigger". Thankfully the ITV London cameras, which were there for the lunchtime news bulletin, weren't in earshot of the assailant.

It was reminiscent of some of the overt abuse and hostility of my childhood, when at times I got abuse for looking like I was from both the Caribbean and Asian diaspora. However, at least people are honest and in terms of homophobia, much more accepting than some middle-class moralists I have met. During an introductory tour of the neighbourhood I was shown the local gay club as if it was just another pub, and even one of the local tenant halls closest to the New Den held regular drag shows during Pride. If they don't like you they'll say so, but if you tell the truth and say yes or no, rather than maybe, they'll respect and welcome you. That's been my experience and I can only relate what has happened to me.

'Sledging' at players by the fans in the way that Son was treated isn't a new occurrence. I remember that Stan Collymore, when he played for Aston Villa, was regularly booed by opposing fans for his arrogance. It hid a tormented mind, as he had problems associated with self-loathing – an angry temperament, bouts of depression and an obsessive nature, especially when it came to sexual gratification. It's exactly the sort of symptoms I displayed before my diagnosis for clinical depression in 1999. It's different from manic depression, where there are extreme highs and lows of behaviour. So I had some affinity with him when I heard that he suffered from this anguish and also I could relate to the awful treatment he was subjected to by his employer, the Villa manager, John Gregory. When I asked my manager for time off when I experienced this at Lewisham in 1998, I was told to pull myself together and shouted at that I would lose my job because of how weak I was. When I heard that Collymore was told the same by Gregory and that someone on his salary shouldn't be depressed, I went on BBC Radio5 Live to express my solidarity, saying that no matter what you're paid, mental health issues can affect anyone, from whatever class or background and without knowing Collymore's experiences, no one could dismiss him in such a way. When you read his autobiography and learn what he has had to endure, you realise that he has had a tough life.

An event in my childhood which still affects me happened on the last day of February 1970. That was when my father was sectioned after a day of drama at our family home in Finchley. They say time heals, but that's not my own experience. When you're younger you tend to block out memories or find coping strategies. Now I feel those memories of a dark, dark day more real and prevailing as an adult, as I appreciate what torment my Dad was enduring. He spent three months in a home and returned to us just as the World Cup that year was drawing to a close.

My own diagnosis came as I dwelt too much on a belief that I would follow the same route as my father, when I approached the age he was in 1970. There's nothing inevitable about madness though, as long as you can express your feelings and have someone to listen to.

The month ended with two England internationals. This time England lost to Germany in a Berlin friendly 1-0, but the English crowd wasn't that friendly at all and sung throughout their national anthem. In the World Cup Qualifier against Lithuania, a few days after, I joined up with fellow LGBT football fans, who were represented in force at the match. The Pride in Football umbrella group for LGBT fan groups now counts 25 such clubs with these in existence, almost doubling the number when I last attended an England match with LGBT fans two years ago. This time there was no abuse or vilification from fellow supporters when we unfurled the rainbow flag for our customary pre-match photo opportunity. As I watched the dreary England performance, it was good to see Jermain Defoe, the Spurs legend, getting a recall, scoring a goal and being awarded man of the match. The crowd this time was more respectful as there was a moment's silence and wreaths were laid on the pitch for the terrorist incident in Westminster a week before, where four people were killed by an Islamist gunman before he was shot dead.

In fact I was pretty impressed with the diversity of the English fans. There were many black and Asian supporters among them – whole families in fact.

Far from the maddening crowd.

It was a month of home wins for Spurs. We began with a 3-2 win against Everton, a score which belied our total dominance in the match, and after pulverising Millwall in the FA Cup we beat Southampton 2-1, which meant that since we lost to the Saints at the Lane last May, we had gone on to win 10 consecutive home matches in the Premiership – a club record. And let's hope we can keep this up until the end of the season, our last in the old stadium.

CHAPTER 31

I'VE GOT ANOTHER SEMI

✳

APRIL 2017

See what I just did there, in the chapter title? It's called a double entendre and without explaining what it means, I am prone to them as a fan of the much-missed Carry On films. If, in a parallel universe, I did get to appear in the world's most prestigious quiz show, BBC's *Mastermind*, the films would be my specialist subject ahead of the Spurs. I like the banter, and some football fans can be quite extraordinarily funny in the chants they sing. So, for example, as we were singing 'We're on our way to Wembley' to the Millwall fans packed into the away end during our quarter-final FA cup tie, they quickly retorted with 'We're on our way to Shrewsbury', which was probably their next League One match.

As we approached the next round, the penultimate of the FA Cup against Chelsea, arguments about where banter becomes plain offensive reared their heads again. Is the chant 'Chelsea rent boys we're coming for you' homophobic? Well Spurs don't seem to think so. When the Proud Lilywhites approached the club about this song a couple of seasons ago, we were told that they view it as an attack on the wealthy nature of the Stamford Bridge outfit, rather than a homophobic slur. This didn't stop Manchester United supporters being reported to the police by disgruntled Chelsea fans after their match at Old Trafford this season.

For me, there's no question about its origins and intent, and the Spurs officials ought to know their history. Chelsea's ground is located in Earls Court, which for many decades in the 20th century was an area of prostitution where men paid for sex with rent boys. Even royal patrons such as the Duke of Clarence, Queen Victoria's grandson, are alleged to have frequented brothels in the area. The pub where I used to bump into Justin Fashanu, the Colherne, is in the neighbourhood and people often used the nearby Brompton Cemetery for cruising and casual sex.

In 1992 I was asked to become a member of the management board of Streetwise Youth, a charity established in Earls Court in 1985 to help rent boys, as young male prostitutes were termed, to avoid the dangers of unsafe sex and drugs. Many of the sex workers came from other regions of the country bedazzled by the openness of

London, and often fleeing from parents who had disowned them because of their sexuality. I helped the charity establish an outreach project, which specifically targeted the growing number of black and minority ethnic sex workers from Africa and the Middle and Far East, who also had issues associated with their asylum status. The charity has now closed and sex workers, rather than operating on the streets, use their own homes or brothels and pickup clients through on-line apps.

So for me this chant, which pre-dates Roman Abramovich taking over Chelsea, is clearly homophobic and demeaning to gay men. Some may find it funny just as the chanting against Brighton and Hove Albion fans is intended to be. However, as I've said, when a whole set of supporters, your own teams' fans, are shouting 'Does your boyfriend know you're here?' or 'We can see you holding hands' it really does isolate you as a gay fan and makes you feel not welcome and more importantly, that you are not worthy to belong to a group supporting Spurs. We shall have to see where the Greater Manchester police service's investigation of the complaint leads.

In the meantime, there has been yet another attempt to challenge homophobia on the terraces after a damning report by the Media, Culture and Sports House of Commons select committee this year. This has led to the launch of a new training kit for stewards who have to deal with such situations on the terraces. Included in this kit is a powerful new film commissioned by Kick it Out. It includes testimony from a black gay West Ham fan, an older gay Arsenal supporter, Sophie Cook and a lesbian steward. I was asked by Sophie to appear on her television programme 'Beyond the Rainbow' to promote the film. The film is great and hopefully shouldn't be used just to train stewards and other football club staff, but be shown before matches to supporters, and even as a commercial on television.

I can't help feeling though that we've been here before. A bit like reforming itself, the Football Association (FA) makes all the right noises about being troubled by the problem of homophobia, but actually once the media storm dies down, it simply turns its attention to something else. The crucial change came in 1997 with an election of Britain's first gay-friendly government with three out Cabinet Ministers. So as laws such as Section 28 were repealed and anti-discrimination legislation enacted, it seemed that there was a wind of change in the air. Things came to a head with Robbie Fowler and Graeme Le Saux in a match at Anfield in October 1999. Whilst Le Saux was about to take a free-kick, Fowler showed his backside to him, trying to provoke a reaction. All it did was to increase the ferocity of the homophobic abuse from the home crowd directed at Graeme Le Saux. The referee did nothing to punish the Liverpool player and for a long time after the occurrence, Fowler failed to apologise to the Chelsea player. I went on Sky Sports News in the week after the match and was interviewed on 'Live at Five'. My point was not so much about how Le Saux merited an apology, but so did the thousands of LGBT supporters from both sides – Chelsea and Liverpool – who were actually at the game or watching the match on television. It never occurred to the interviewer that there would actually be LGBT football fans who were deeply offended and felt ostracised by Fowler's actions that day.

In response, in February 2000, the FA said that they were enlisting the help of Stonewall, the country's leading LGBT group, to establish a campaign directed at the rights of gay players and supporters. The campaign would include a commercial being made to be shown in cinemas and on television, the training of young footballers, posters in grounds and statements in match day programmes. I was also quoted in *The Guardian* by my friend and fellow Spurs fan Vivek Chaudray on the issue. I saw no posters in stadiums and very little mention of homophobia in programmes. There may have been training in diversity for footballers, but clearly what was needed was training for all staff, including managers and training coaches. As for the commercial, it was made but the launch was stalled, as the FA could not find one England international player who was willing to be associated with it. Presumably they thought that they would be falsely associated with being gay, in the way Le Saux was treated. I did recall seeing the commercial in the cinema and although it didn't mention homophobia, it did depict a good argument about how offensive behaviour wouldn't be tolerated anywhere else other than a football pitch. As I said at the time abuse "really makes you question whether you should support your team and whether you should be involved in football at all". This was quite prescient given the abuse Le Saux had to endure, and we had to hear, as I have already covered, from supporters sitting next to us for his next away match as at White Hart Lane.

Ten years later, before the start of the 2009-10 season, Stonewall published a report jointly with the GFSN. This time GFSN had followed Brighton and Hove Albion for a whole season, detailing some of the homophobia their supporters had to endure at every game. Of course most of these fans, like Le Saux, weren't gay, but they still fell prey to homophobic insults. This time the report was front-page news and I was quoted in a story which made all the tabloids, including the *Metro*, as I spoke about the homophobic incident we endured at Coventry City, which I have mentioned earlier. This time the red carpet was rolled out to GFSN and a delegation was invited to a Downing Street summit by the incoming Prime Minister of a coalition government, David Cameron. For my part, although I welcomed this, the advent of social media now meant that the abuse had developed into something more sinister.

On one chat forum, supposedly for West Ham 'fans' called Bubble Blowers, I was targeted for my comments. One said that I spent all my time hanging around toilets looking for sex during matches, which was bizarre, as the writer clearly believed that maybe there are other gay fans! The only gay men's fan group at the time, the Pink Lions, supporters of Millwall, came under attack from the same site. This led to the Millwall Anti-Racist Trust changing its focus to include other issues aligned with discrimination and altering the name of the Trust to 'Millwall for All'. I also discovered that someone had set up a Facebook account in my name and was using it to promote homophobia.

At least this time there was a response from clubs and the authorities, which included changes to ground regulations in an attempt outlaw homophobic chanting. Clubs also begun to promote the idea of LGBT supporters' groups, with Arsenal becoming the first Premiership team to launch one: the Gay Gooners.

Chelsea have set up their own LGBT fan club this season, although they haven't come up with a name as yet that plays with a possible double entendre with their location on the Kings Road!

As we prepared to meet the Blues, I was praying that seven really was a lucky number, for we had lost all the previous six since that special day in 1991 when Gazza stormed Arsenal. If we were to lose a seventh consecutive semi-final it would be historic in terms of the FA Cup. Only one other club had equalled our present record of six and that was, ironically, Chelsea. I missed the first losing semi-final in 1993, when we played the Gooners again – a bit like London buses, you wait a hundred years for one North London semi-final derby and then two come along within the space of three years! Thankfully I had pre-booked a holiday in the windy city of Chicago that year, my first trip to the USA, so I didn't have to see the Gooners winning.

Two years later we played Everton at Elland Road. Spurs had done well to get that far after originally being denied entry to the competition as a sanction for irregular payments during the Venables regime. We had gone to court to get that and a 12-point deduction in the League overturned. The FA therefore were in no mood to do us favours and placed all Spurs fans at one end of the stadium, meaning that three sides were packed with Merseyside supporters. It felt as if we were playing away and with an injured Darren Anderton in the side, who clearly wasn't up for it, we lost badly, 4-1.

I actually went to the final that year and the one before and after it, compliments of a friend at the English Schools FA who had a spare ticket. I was shocked when Daniel

Amokachi, Everton's first black player since 1976, was called a 'black bastard' by one of their own fans when he missed a chance to score. Everyone looked at me and nodded their heads as if to say sorry. I did, for the first time, have enough courage to stand and challenge the supporter. Without looking at me, he apologised by saying that he didn't really mean it.

In 1999 we met Newcastle United at Old Trafford and went out 2-0 to the Magpies, and two years later were back at the same ground to lose to Woolwich 3-1. That match marked Sol Campbell's last game before he defected to the other side, and due to the 'Bosman ruling', Arsenal didn't have to pay us a transfer fee. I've already told you about our miserable form at Wembley, which started with that awful defeat against Portsmouth in 2010 and then again two years later the 5-1 mauling by Chelsea. Maybe all I can hope for is to have another semi in two years' time!

This year's match was real end-to-end stuff, with both teams playing at full throttle. It surprised me that Poch had changed the team selection, preferring Son in a wing-back role to Kyle Walker, who remained on the bench. We paid the penalty, as although we had levelled through Harry Kane, after a Willian opener for Chelsea, Son gave away a penalty just before half-time to the Blues. Willian scored the second so Chelsea led 2-1 at half-time. Yet the Spurs team which came out for the second half was not the one that came out against the Blues in 2012, our last semi-final in this competition, and we didn't fold this time around. Eriksen, who had played in Kane for our first, had another assist for Dele Alli to score our equaliser and we were all over them – like the proverbial rash. Unfortunately it was

Antonio Conte, the Italian Head Coach, who had the ace card and played it; he brought on Hazard as a substitute and he immediately scored a third goal. Chelsea eventually won 4-2.

I wish someone had told me that we had won seven semis in the FA Cup between 1961, when we won the double, and that one against the Gooners in 1991, which upset their double plans. So I suppose it makes some symmetrical sense that we should then lose the next seven! The last times we have won a trophy also seems to follow a mathematical pattern, with one more year to wait each time: 1984/91/99/2008. So I should have not expected another trophy win until next season.

Chelsea's double plan was still on course then, despite our solid League form. In the Premiership we beat Burnley and Swansea City away followed by Watford and Bournemouth at the Lane, which meant we had gone seven league games without losing – a club record.

CHAPTER 32

THE LAST TABOO

✳

APRIL/MAY 2017

The disappointment of another semi-final calamity was followed by two tricky London derbies in the Premiership. We edged out Crystal Palace in the first 1-0 at Selhurst Park, and played Arsenal in our penultimate home match of the season.

Before the match, I had been approached by the producers of a BBC television documentary to be called 'How homophobic is football?' It was being made by BBC Wales to commemorate the 50th anniversary of the decriminalisation of homosexuality in England and Wales next year and would be fronted by an out football player – a professional, no less, who had played a distinguished international career for Wales. The only problem was that he played with the wrong shape of ball. He was Gareth Thomas, the former Welsh Rugby Union and League professional. Thomas came out in December 2009 and exactly a year later, Fraser and I met him at a friend's 60th birthday party. Gareth was passionate about gay rights and how he felt that he could influence others to come out and to campaign against homophobia in sport. He seemed in awe of us for spending 25 years as out gay men on the football terraces. He admitted that because of his own prejudices about masculinity he had thought the LGBT community wouldn't be interested in football, and he had been stopped from being honest to himself and others around him by the fear of rejection and hostility from players and supporters alike.

So when he got in contact again, I suggested he should film us with the Proud Lilywhites just before the derby match against the Woolwich. Appropriately enough we were filmed in the Pride of Tottenham pub on the High Street. It was clear from the onset that Gareth had lost none of his passion for being a positive role model and he didn't refrain from asking us difficult questions, which I had been mindful of when writing this book. For starters he commended the recent growth of LGBT fan clubs and wondered why, if these were now in place, footballers still did not come out. He knew several who still feared the rejection, particularly by their own fans, if they revealed their sexuality. Despite our visibility, with the rainbow flag prominent at home matches and at the Football v Homophobia match, with players wearing T-shirts campaigning for our cause, there were still no footballers who were prepared to take that final step. Where we were going wrong?

I was glad that most of those there stated that the problem was fear, and like many fears, it was unfounded and purely speculative. We said that the issue wasn't with supporters now but with the authorities, the chairmen, who were of another generation, or the players who participated in dressing room banter and above all the FA, which had recently said that there would be a detrimental reaction by supporters to out gay football professionals. This doesn't set the right tone and appeared, as ever, to put the blame on football's ills on the supporters. We retorted that now, as opposed to say when Fashanu came out, every supporter who goes to a game knows someone who is out, whether it's a family member, a friend, a neighbour or a work colleague. Things had changed, but football hadn't, in many respects, kept up.

Gareth spoke about the wall of silence he was getting from the football governing bodies about the issue while filming this documentary. Not a single Premiership club had wanted to go on camera talking about the issue, and they still hadn't persuaded a footballer, gay or straight, to talk about it. He forlornly said that he couldn't see a player coming out soon. I drew some parallels with the racist reaction to black players in the 1970s and 80s and said that they had the strength of character and purpose to play despite the monkey chants, the bananas thrown onto the pitch and the odd comment from other players, so surely we were being too pessimistic about gay footballers being able to do the same.

Gareth wrapped up the conversation by asking us why, despite all the campaigns like Football v Homophobia, homophobic insults were still heard at matches. I said that he was right to pick up on this and that at first Kick it Out, when confronting racism, had still had the same brick wall mentality facing it, and in many respects still does. For example Liverpool players wore Kick it Out training apparel a few weeks before they wore T-shirts supporting Luis Suarez, was found guilty of making a racist remark to Manchester United's Patrice Evra. Wearing badges and T-shirts once a season, although it's important and focuses attention, doesn't change attitudes and behaviour for the rest of the season.

We all agreed with Gareth's notion of an ongoing educational campaign that would be highly visible, such as UEFA's Respect campaign, where commercials are shown before and after matches on television and at match day screens, with top elite footballers saying that homophobia has no place in the sport. I said that only when Gareth Thomas could have a discussion with the fans who weren't like us wearing Proud Lilywhites badges would we be effecting change in attitudes and behaviour. Not one England international or prominent Premiership player could be enticed either by the FA or PFA to front such a campaign, and to admit that terms used in the dressing room, seen as banter, such as 'faggot', 'poof' or 'gay boy', prevented some players being open about who they are.

As the TV cameras followed us with Gareth Thomas to the ground, there was an unnerving heavy police presence, because the last North London derby in our old stadium had clearly been a target for some bad behaviour. I speculated that if even if we did all the things we were talking about, the sheer masculinity and tribalism of the sport of football might be a deterrent to someone coming out. I also asked the producer of the documentary why he hadn't taken up my offer to film Gareth inside the ground, as we had a spare ticket and he could have joined us to hear some of the reactions to comments by us to anything that might be said, particularly as this was a derby match, where such comments could be heard. Apparently Spurs had said no, and in a nutshell that was the problem with having an officially-recognised supporters' group like the Proud Lilywhites. There was only so far you could go and you could certainly not do or show anything that might be detrimental to the club. I said that if the budget allowed it, they should go to countries where LGBT fans weren't campaigning in isolation and have them join up with other supporters, unfurling stadium banners for tolerance and understanding.

In another terrific performance we took our unbeaten run to nine matches and played the Gunners off the pitch. Remembering a couple of seasons ago when we had had a stall at the derby match against the Gunners and won, I thought that maybe campaigning against homophobia for this match at least, might affect the result in our favour. We won 2-0 with goals from Alli and Kane, who were fast becoming the best young striking partnership in the country. That boded well for both club and country.

One of the comments made at our pre-match meeting with Gareth got me thinking. It was from our youngest member in the Proud Lilywhites, who, in his early 20s, had just finished a vocational course in youth work. He thought that maybe we were going for the wrong audience in our battle to reveal the last taboo in football. It won't be registered players where one comes out, but the academy or reserves where under-23s play, he felt. Given, that unlike when I was at school, many people are coming out in their late teens in an environment that is now, in most places, more supportive to young people questioning their sexuality, shouldn't we be campaigning for youth, academy and development coaches to be supportive of LGBT players being open? So when these players progress further, there won't be an issue surrounding their sexuality.

As I have stated before, the professional men's game now has 5,000 players registered. The rule of thumb would be that one in 10 has had experiences of a gay or bisexual nature, according to the Kinsey scale. However, more recent monitoring has shown that only about 1.5% of the population identify as being LGBT, so perhaps that narrows the field to about 75. However, because of what we have heard about the dressing room banter and avowed masculinity amongst footballers, maybe gay footballers don't become professionals and are either channelled out by clubs wary of their ability to be strong on the pitch, or they leave by choice, as they get weary of the discrimination they endure. That still leaves us with a reasonable guess that you could, at the very least, be talking about 26 players being gay or bisexual in the professional game right now. That's the size of an international squad.

One such former player did discuss with me his reasons for quitting the professional game, and he's the first footballer prepared to become a patron of an LGBT supporters group. He made it professionally to the reserves of Bradford City FC, who are currently in the League One play-off final at Wembley against Millwall, for a place in the Championship next season. Adam McCabe grew up in Florida and as a 13-year-old went to Argentina, where he played regularly against teams from Boca Juniors and River Plate. He left the USA at 19 for an English university, Leeds, as part of an exchange programme. Whilst he was studying for a degree in International Business, he was scouted by Bradford City and offered a place in their under-21 team. He made the reserve team about a dozen times. Unfortunately he fell suspect to a chronic illness, ulcerative colitis, which cut short his promising career. It was the same illness that affected Darren Fletcher. He also told me however, that the mental anguish he went through in having to hide his sexuality from fellow team mates and the club also played a part. Whilst playing for the team or sitting it out on the bench waiting for a call up to the reserve team, he was always anxious and afraid that his sexuality would be revealed, and that it would be a distraction from his profession. He thought that if had come out at that stage of his football career, it would have affected his selection in the team. This was because he had to endure all sorts of negative comments about being gay. He's surprisingly not aggrieved by those who made these comments, as he believes that they were only using terminology that they had always heard in their own careers and that derogatory terms like 'faggot' or 'fairy' were used to motivate and inspire teams, particularly just before they played. They weren't used directly at a particular person, but nonetheless McCabe thought that if he told them he was a gay, then his own place in the team might be put in jeopardy.

This was heightened by the fact that in one of the teams

he played for, one of the back room staff was gay and out to the players. However, this didn't stop his team mates making offensive comments once this member of staff left the dressing room. What his team mates thought was banter, saying that they were glad the person wasn't around when they took a shower, for example, clearly affected Adam, so much so that he became hypersensitive to saying anything that might be construed as admitting he was gay. Again it's an example of footballers not even thinking that someone who was gay would be in their own team and probably something they had always expressed at school and college that had gone unchallenged and unreported.

The chronic illness led to Adam taking a break from Bradford City. He rehabilitated in the USA and decided to stay there, and he is now successfully playing at a semi-professional level in the fourth tier of football, and is out and open. So much so that he became patron to the LGBT Bradford City supporters group, the first such footballer to do so. He says now that he wants to be a mentor to any young player who is struggling with coming to terms with being open about his own sexuality and afraid of disclosing this to the outside world. When he was a professional, there was only Robbie Rogers, who had already left Leeds United to play in the Major Soccer League in the USA, that he could turn to. He makes a crucial point here: that in each team and in every club there needs to be a mentor, an ambassador for the younger players, to act as their confidant.

How many players would come forward to fill this role? One would think that in a 'metrosexual' world where some men are actually comfortable with others fancying them this would be easier. However, not every dressing room has a

David Beckham or Joey Barton, one suspects. In moving the debate against homophobia from the behaviour of supporters to the attitudes held in the boardroom and more especially, the dressing room, I believe we will be more adept in fighting against the last taboo. It is in the dressing room and on the pitch where players bond, partnerships are met and regardless of which club they play for, friendships for the length of their respective careers are made.

It was into this intense environment full of cliques that a Jersey-born footballer entered when he joined Chelsea. In his own words "Because I had different interests, because I didn't feel comfortable in the laddish drinking culture that was prevalent in English football...it was generally assumed by my team mates that there was something wrong with me. It followed naturally that I must be gay." Rumours about players' sexuality seem, certainly in this case, not to have been the notion of some media hack looking for a story, but based on assumptions made by players, which are then leaked out of the club, one way or another. It is galling to hear from Graeme Le Saux that he was targeted by some of his own players, simply because he didn't fit in. According to his testimony, it all started in 1991 and would hang over his career for 14 years. Those who bantered in the dressing room assumed that Le Saux must be gay simply because he preferred camping to hotel holidays, read newspapers such as *The Guardian* rather than the sports pages of the tabloids and wore student clothes rather than the latest fashion from the Kings Road. So Le Saux had no mentor to turn to, no one to confide in when he was bullied and harassed, and when the rumours leaked out of the dressing room and onto the terraces, he had to endure abuse from spectators and other players alike. Even the coaches turned on Graeme, and he says that one of them would regularly call him a poof. This was all at the same time that Fashanu had come out, a player whose career soon fell apart through ridicule and abuse. Le Saux thought his would suffer similarly, and so it played out with the Robbie Fowler incident I have already covered. That was also much more painful as it was the first match his wife brought their newly-born daughter to.

At home against Liverpool, a fellow England international paid no penalty for calling him a poof and asking him if he took it up the arse. Le Saux says that the referee on that day could have made a point of sending Fowler off for misconduct, which would have sent a strong message out to others that homophobia wasn't acceptable. Terry Durkin avoided doing that and instead booked Le Saux for complaining, contesting that he was time wasting! Le Saux was actually fined by the FA and given a one-match ban. Fowler was fined more and suffered harsher match bans, but he had exacerbated the situation by mocking cocaine-snorting after he scored, as part of a goal celebration. He got four matches for that whilst it was only two matches for the homophobic incident involving showing his backside to Le Saux and asking him to give him one up the arse. Clearly the FA has their priorities misplaced, to say the least.

Le Saux believed at the time that the abuse and vitriol he suffered from fellow players would be enough to persuade gay players not to come out or even prevent straight footballers like himself from supporting campaigns against homophobia. Incidentally, Le Saux wasn't one of these; he had the courage and strength to speak out about the behaviour he had to tolerate and how the environment it created was homophobic.

'Guilty by association' drives many players therefore to turn their backs on supporting anti-homophobia campaigns. For example, despite asking, no Premiership players seems able to utter the words 'it's fine to be gay' when asked to front initiatives such as the Football v Homophobia campaign. Wearing T-shirts or smiling at rainbow flags in the stadium is OK, but uttering a few sentences is beyond their reach – they would rather be silent. Even when the Gooners launched a video in support of Stonewall's rainbow laces campaign, which asks players to don the apparel for one match, although the laces were prominent and it was clear what was being supported – 'to be different is fine' – there was still no mention of the word 'gay'. It's a great video by the way, don't get me wrong, as it's set in a dressing room and a shirtless Giroud says he can't help being gorgeous, but it still doesn't quite cross that last taboo.

I did notice that when Giroud played against us there were some ugly comments, obviously from ugly people who were envious of his Gallic good looks. However, it shows that even appearing in a video may make a player an easy target for abuse. So it really needs a whole-club approach in my view, not just the dressing room but the management in the dugout and chairmen and women on the board. No one should feel isolated or ostracised if a similar player to Le Saux faces the innuendo today.

After the win against Arsenal there was no let up in the derbies' schedule as we went off to the London Stadium to play the Hammers. With Chelsea still only four points ahead of us in the Premiership, it was important for us to register our ninth League win on the trot. Significantly, we also remained unbeaten at home since pulling back a victory from the jaws of defeat when West Ham visited us in November, winning 3-2. and since then we have won the last 13 home Premiership matches. The Hammers themselves were flirting with relegation so we could be expectant of a hard-fought game – both on and off the pitch.

Ahead of the match I couldn't help but recalling an incident from ten years previously. Known as 'lasagnegate', it was the last match of the 2005-06 season, when we played at Upton Park. We needed a win to beat the Gooners to a place in the Champions League by ending up fourth in the table. However, a pre-match meal of lasagne led to most of our team suffering from food poisoning, including our talisman, Edgar Davids. We lost the game 2-1 and blew our chances of clinching a Champions League spot. Many blamed the possibility of a Woolwich-supporting chef in the hotel where the players had eaten their Italian meal.

An investigation later claimed that it was a virus that had affected the players, which had spread through the team. Whatever the problem was, it meant that we had to wait another four years to succeed in getting into the European elite. I had decided to forfeit my ticket for the match and held a get-together in my house in Barking afterwards. I had been shattered by the result of the local council elections a couple of nights before, where I had worked my guts out for a Labour victory. I lost that one as well, as 11 BNP councillors had been elected. Thankfully they hadn't stood in every ward, so Labour still controlled the borough, but if they had done then the storm troopers of the far-right would have invaded the Town Hall. I was too upset and had an eerie feeling that Spurs would blow it on the day, although I wasn't expecting such an occurrence to happen. One small gesture did help to overcome the sense of failure because Davids gave his shirt to Fraser, who has since framed it, and it now hangs on his bedroom wall with the Dutch players' DNA intact. It would be his and Michael Carrick's last game for us.

If one footballer came out and then another, wouldn't there be constant speculation that they were dating each other? Le Saux was matched up with Ken Monkou by his team mates, simply because they shared a tent on a camping holiday. I've heard rumours about all sorts of affairs, none of which I can repeat. Maybe they start in the dressing room and then leak out, gaining substance or being altered. One such rumour affected West Ham and travelled so far that the club had to put out a statement saying that if it was repeated in a newspaper or by the media, they would sue for defamation of character. However, it was repeated so often on-line that it is now part of common currency amongst the football fraternity. It was alleged (and I use that word not to assume that any crime was in fact made) that Hammers striker Trevor Morley had been caught in the act with his team mate Ian Bishop by his wife in 2000. Morley alleges that the rumour was started by his aggrieved spouse, who he had divorced after she stabbed him. He says the allegations ruined his career and he had to play with taunts coming from his own fans. I do recall that when the two of them played together at Spurs, whenever one touched the ball, the crowd as one suddenly became very camp and whistled whilst others spouted out the usual taunts. For his part, Ian Bishop claims that his international career never took off because of the rumours. Whether or not any of it is true, it just goes to show how quickly rumours can spread. One footnote to this story; whilst I was working in Barking and on one of the most deprived estates in the country, the Gascoigne (not named in commemoration of Gazza), I was told a slightly different version, which involved a youth player who came from the estate and a romance with a first-team player at the Boleyn.

Some footballers have put their heads above the parapet to show their solidarity with the cause, most notable David Beckham, who has often talked about his positive attitude to gay men. He was the first footballer to do a photo-shoot for the gay magazine *Attitude* and his provocative adverts for male underwear are certainly shot with a view to appealing to the 'pink pound'. He was followed by Freddie Ljungberg, the Gooners' Swedish international, and then in 2003 by West Ham's Matt Jarvis. The first two had lucrative modelling careers, but for the Boleyn boy there was only grief. As soon as he appeared, despite having a wife, rumours began circulating that Jarvis was gay. None of the three seemed to mind rumours about their sexuality and all are married. It is remarkable that posing for photo-shoots aimed at a male audience didn't seem to affect any of their careers and at least with the first two, they clearly benefited financially.

It's not so easy if you're single. In 2004 Matt Taylor, who also played for the Hammers, was linked to the winner of the ITV talent show *Pop Idol*, Will Young. Taylor was thought of as an England international and he states that his form suffered due to all the innuendo, which was more virulent on the internet chat rooms than on the terraces. That cannot be said of Sol Campbell. The ex-Spurs player was regularly abused with offensive chants, one of which talked about his HIV status and being hanged from a tree. This climaxed in one match in 2009 when Campbell, now playing with Portsmouth after years at Woolwich, was the subject of sustained barracking about his sex life from the Spurs supporters. This came from an article circulating in the Sunday newspapers that three black players had engaged in a sex act, which had been filmed. For the first time, two fans were found guilty of homophobic chanting and a further 13 supporters were charged with racist chanting. The use of closed circuit cameras was vital in providing irrefutable evidence and the reverberations led to Spurs being the first club to specifically outlaw homophobic chanting in the club's ground regulations.

There is something that links Ljungberg, Taylor, Jarvis, Morley and Bishop with Thomas Hitzlsperger, and it's not their sexuality – it's the fact that they all played for West Ham sometime during their footballing careers. There must be something in the soil at the Boleyn. On the field, Spurs lost to the Hammers by a solitary goal and this effectively ended the slim hopes of us catching up Chelsea in the race for the Premiership. Crucially though we would now end a run of 22 years of the Gooners ending the season above us, and we had confirmed our Champions League place for next season.

As we have seen, it's not just gay players that are taunted; those who are said to act gay or those where unfounded rumours start and flourish can also be victims of homophobic abuse. To tackle homophobia, we should be all-inclusive. By that I mean we shouldn't always be looking for the first player to come out before addressing the issue or running to his assistance like an ambulance service once he's come out. We have to address the issue now, as players are being affected, and not just players but of course the visible LGBT supporters and their allies who attend matches. We all know someone close to us who is gay, and we'd all be affected if that person was subjected to the abuse that masquerades as banter, at say where they work. When I first started going to Spurs, we weren't all affected by it and we couldn't all empathise with the issue, but a welcome result of more people being out is that that situation has changed.

So make no assumptions. I am as guilty as most people are in that respect. For the many seasons that we sat together in the East Stand, on the side of us were many Jewish fans. At one match I noticed that the man next to Fraser had brought an older man with him, whom I believed was his father. As I got up to go for a half-time break I said to him, "Nice to see you that your dad likes the Spurs as well as you." To which he replied, "Oh he's not my dad, he's my partner, and he doesn't know the first thing about football." For nigh on 15 years we had been sitting next to Elliot, as we later found he was called, and I never envisaged that he was gay. He had cottoned on that we were gay and his Jewish friends sitting next to him all knew he was. In a crowd of 36,000 people, don't assume who is or who isn't affected by homophobia.

And don't think that you know what being gay looks like. On one occasion we were playing QPR and I had agreed to meet my best friend, Peter, the one who worked at the

Foreign Office and is a Rangers fan, with his other straight friends in a pub after the game. Obviously we didn't wear any colours, but as we walked into the pub, they all took a second look at us and you could see by their reaction that they thought we looking for trouble. We were all pretty glum, as we had just lost the match 4-1 at Loftus Road, as their stadium was called. It wasn't until we sat down and began chatting that any tension in the air subsided.

Afterwards I phoned my friend Peter and asked why his mates were a bit scared of us. "Surely they didn't think we were going to cause trouble?" I said.

"Well yes they did," he replied. "They thought you were a bunch of skinheads, dressed in your bomber jackets and with short cropped hair."

My brother tells a similar story. When he used to walk to games from the tube at Earls Court, he'd often cross through Brompton Cemetery on his way to Stamford Bridge. A number of times he was amazed at the amount of skinheads in the cemetery and thought it might be a meeting point for fascist sympathisers. Those were the days when the National Front sold their weekly newspaper outside grounds, so he had every right to make this assumption. I laughed out loud when he told me and said he shouldn't worry as it was gay skinheads cruising, because the cemetery near the Colherne pub, where I used to meet Justin, was a notorious pick-up point.

Players ought to be in the forefront of stamping out any homophobia that comes from professionals on the pitch, or the training ground or dressing room. They are all work environments after all, and such behaviour is outlawed elsewhere by employment legislation on bullying and harassment. In many respects, the PFA, the players' trades union, is in the envious position of being a closed shop. It certainly has the capacity and strength to, for example, suspend any player from membership, put pressure on clubs when coaches make derogatory comments, and in extreme scenarios call for strike action if no effective sanctions are taken, for example, when crowds victimise a particular player during matches. This last sanction has been called for by Garth Crooks to deal with racist chanting, if it goes unpunished by referees during a game. Recently, Sulley Montari, who plays in the Italian League, was sent-off from a game after remonstrating with the referee that he wasn't taking any notice of the racist chanting directed to him. He was even given a one-match ban for his red card, which was later rescinded. In extreme situations, I think players should effectively be allowed to withdraw their labour. So the PFA need to have a plan of action in place now and not just wait for the first footballer to come out before addressing the issue.

The authorities, from the FA right down through the Premier League and those clubs beyond, should do two things. Firstly, equalities and diversity training should be mandatory for anyone connected with football: players, officials, stewards, staff, managers and coaches. You shouldn't wait for a player to make an offensive comment before sending them on a mandatory training course. The second thing is to campaign not just for one month or at one match on the issue of homophobia in football, but to have a comprehensive awareness-raising programme throughout the whole game, which uses all forms of media. A slice of the new television deal the Premiership clubs have extracted from the broadcasters, the richest such contract in the world, should be used to advertise the message on television, in cinemas and before and after matches. Respect has been the campaign in UEFA but I would like a similar one that tackles homophobia directly and shows footballers as role models saying no to discrimination. There are some great examples out there that I have already mentioned, such as the Millwall for All and Football v Homophobia film and the new training video being used by Kick it Out, but there must be no excuses used, as I have noted before, that they couldn't get a footballer to front it or they haven't enough money to sustain it. As far as I'm concerned, after stop starting anti-homophobia campaigns on at least three occasions since Justin took his life, the FA is the last-chance saloon.

So for me, inclusiveness, training and campaigning are important, and if these aren't successful, the ultimate use of sanctions. And I don't mean just fines, but stadium bans as a first resort for perpetrators in the stands and automatic suspensions for players on the pitch. Isolate the homophobes – not the gay supporters or players. Finally, LGBT fan clubs, at 30 and rising as I conclude this book, need to learn lessons from those I have met abroad. They need to join up with other supporters' campaigns, like those welcoming refugees or those promoting women's participation. Good as the rainbow flag is flying in a corner of White Hart Lane, I won't feel totally happy until I'm at a match where the banner is being unfurled by fans on the side of the stadium where I sit. Then, and only then, would I be able to fully appreciate that we have broken down the last taboo.

It is rather apt that this book closes with the last season at White Hart Lane before the old stadium is totally knocked down and a new one, with a much larger capacity of 61,000 replaces it. That won't be ready until 2018-19 at the earliest, so for next season and maybe the one after that, Wembley Stadium will stage our home matches in the Premier League and cup competitions. I can't be too sentimental about the old stadium as we're not moving home from Tottenham, just upgrading to a better home. And whatever commercial sponsor that gets naming rights, I think it will always be referred to as the Lane.

Our last match was particularly poignant as those around me may not be sitting with us when we return to the new stadium in 2018. For me, Fraser, David, and Vince however, wherever we may have to sit, we will be out as four gay men, and saying that we should still be here.

Unlike last season when we capitulated, Spurs didn't stumble after going out of the title race. We beat Manchester United in our last home game 2-1, which was followed by an emotional closing ceremony for the old ground. We were unbeaten in the league at home for the first time since 1965 and had 14 consecutive home wins in the premiership for the first time ever. In our last two matches, both away, we slaughtered. Leicester City 6-1, last season's champions and went one better by beating Hull City, 7-1, who were already relegated. And for the first time since 1963, we came 2nd in the top flight. Harry Kane won the golden boot for the second consecutive season, scoring his 100th goal for the club.

APPENDIX

✳

TIMELINE – A SUMMARY OF THE MOST MEMORABLE MATCHES

14/11/1978: Home to Nottingham Forest in the FL (lose 3-1) – my first match watching Spurs tarnished by homophobic chanting against Brian Clough.

14/03/1979: Away to Manchester United in the FA Cup QF replay (lose 2-0) – I am outed at homewhilst watching Sportsnight.

23/05/1984: Home to Anderlecht in the UEFA Cup Final (win 4-3 on penalties) – my most memorable home match.

25/08/1990: Home to Manchester City in the FL (win 3-1) – my first game with GFSN as an out fan, just a week after my 26th birthday.

16/01/1991: Away to Chelsea in the FLC (draw 0-0) – at the onset of the 1st Gulf War.

17/08/1992: Away to Southampton in the EPL (win 3-2) – see Take That on stage performing in a gay venue.

07/03/1993: Away to Manchester City in the FA Cup QF (win 4-2) – get beaten-up after the match.

14/08/1993: Away to Newcastle United in the EPL (win 1-0) – my friend is outed by our presence.

29/01/1994: Away to Ipswich Town in the FA Cup 4th Round replay (lose 3-0) – I'm called for on the tannoy.

20/08/1994: Away to Sheffield Wednesday in the EPL (win 4-3) – meet a Spurs player in a gay pub.

11/03/1995: Away to Liverpool in the FA Cup QF (win 2-1) – I score on the way up to the match.

19/02/1996: Away to Nottingham Forest in the FA Cup QF (match abandoned) – follow the Spurs team coach home.

06/12/1997: Home to Chelsea in the EPL (lost 6-1) – worst home match.

10/05/1999: Home to Chelsea in the EPL (draw 2-2) – sickened by the homophobic chanting against Graeme Le Saux.

04/01/2003: Away to Southampton in the FA Cup 3rd round (lose 4-0) – worst away match.

07/05/2006: Away to West Ham United in the EPL (lose 2-1) – lasagnegate

23/11/2006: Away to Bayer Leverkusen in the EL (win 1-0) – meet my childhood hero Martin Chivers.

07/01/2007: Away to Cardiff City in the FA Cup 3rd round (draw 0-0) – get kettled by the police.

05/04/2007: Away to Seville in the UEFA Cup QF (lose 2-1) – nearly get battered by the police.

25/10/2007: Home to Getafe in the UEFA Cup (lose 2-1) – Martin Jol is sacked by text during the match and I vent my anger on ITV London News.

24/02/2008: FLC Final at Wembley vs. Chelsea (win 2-1) – I challenge homophobia.

17/10/2009: Away to Portsmouth in the EPL (win 2-1) – first arrests for homophobic chanting.

07/08/2010: Home to Fiorentina in a friendly (win 3-2) – my first match back in the closet.

20/10/2010: Away to Inter-Milan in the UEFA CL (lose 4-3) – most memorable away match.

30/07/2011: Away to Brighton and Hove Albion in a friendly (win 3-2) – have to endure homophobic chanting.

22/11/2012: Away to Lazio in the UEFA EL (draw 0-0) – meet the Spurs squad in the Sistine Chapel.

27/02/2014: Home to Dnipro in the UEFA EL (win 3-1) – the launch of the Proud Lilywhites.

ACKNOWLEDGEMENTS

I suppose I need to start right at the beginning by giving my heartfelt thanks to Mum and Dad, who made the momentous decision to come to Britain in 1968, when I was a four-year-old. Much of what I have become since is due to the country I live in, love and will grow old in: Great Britain.

My love for writing and reading was nurtured and given scope to blossom at my primary school by teachers whose names I still remember with fondness today: Messrs Snodgrass, Couzens, Shurmer and Tyrell, whose Friday morning writing sessions I devoured and looked forward to the whole of the week.

To my uncle and aunt, Roque and Lillian De Mello, who between them bought my first football annuals, the Rothman's bible and the FA Yearbook: you both began a compulsive obsession for the game I couldn't play but loved to watch.

And to Brian Moore and the Big Match team, my favourite football highlights programme on one of the best TV channels – LWT, who allowed me to take a weekly pew on the terraces.

Then to my brother. He committed me to England and failed with Chelsea, but still loves me and smiles every time we win (unless it's against Chelsea), something I am too proud and vain to do in return.

My love to David, Fraser and Vince. I remember meeting them as I walked into the Salmon and Compasses and wondering in astonishment that there were other gay football fans like me.

To the Gay Football Supporters Network and more recently the Pride in Football group, for their continuing support.

In terms of writing, my thanks to Mitch for the title and agreeing with me that winning the 1984 UEFA Cup Final, whilst standing together on the Shelf, remains the perfect home match we've ever witnessed. To my best friend, Peter, thanks for putting up with being reminded of this book almost daily and not saying that no one would be interested in reading it when he obviously thought so.

To dear Jane Lythell and Adam Powey, two fellow Spurs fans and incredible authors of distinction in their own right, for giving their precious time to advise, assist and mentor me whilst writing.

To Paul Macey, Vivek Chaudary, Anthony Clavane and Chas Newkey-Burden, football writing gods, for their kind considerations and wise words of support.

Special thanks to Adam McCabe, whose insight as a gay footballer was invaluable to me.

Finally, none of this would have been possible if I hadn't fallen in love with the Spurs from White Hart Lane. At times you have infuriated me, made me cry in desperation, drawn tears of joy from me when we won, and in return, at all times you have had my loyalty, love and affection. Writing this book would not have been possible without you and the glory, glory days and nights at the Lane.

Darryl Telles - May 2017